High-Performance Computing Opportunities and Challenges for Army R&D

Robert H. Anderson, Amado Cordova,

Anthony C. Hearn, Rosalind Lewis,

John Matsumura, Isaac R. Porche III,

Randall Steeb

Prepared for the United States Army

Approved for public release; distribution unlimited

RAND ARROYO CENTER

The research described in this report was sponsored by the United States Army under Contract No. DASW01-01-C-0003.

Library of Congress Cataloging-in-Publication Data

Anderson, Robert H. (Robert Helms), 1939-
   High performance computing opportunities and challenges for Army R&D / Robert Anderson, Amado Cordova, Anthony C. Hearn ... [et al.].
      p. cm.
   "TR-310."
   Includes bibliographical references.
   ISBN 0-8330-3888-5 (pbk.)
   1. Military research—United States. 2. United States. Army—Automation. 3. United States. Army—Data processing. 4. High performance computing—United States. I. Cordova, Amado. II. Hearn, Anthony C.. III. Title.

U393.5.A64 2006
355'.070285—dc22

2005036588

The RAND Corporation is a nonprofit research organization providing objective analysis and effective solutions that address the challenges facing the public and private sectors around the world. RAND's publications do not necessarily reflect the opinions of its research clients and sponsors.

RAND® is a registered trademark.

Published 2006 by the RAND Corporation
1776 Main Street, P.O. Box 2138, Santa Monica, CA 90407-2138
1200 South Hayes Street, Arlington, VA 22202-5050
201 North Craig Street, Suite 202, Pittsburgh, PA 15213-1516
RAND URL: http://www.rand.org/
To order RAND documents or to obtain additional information, contact
Distribution Services: Telephone: (310) 451-7002;
Fax: (310) 451-6915; Email: order@rand.org

Preface

This is the final project report of a one-year study entitled "Future High Performance Computing Opportunities for Army Science and Technology," prepared for the Army's Director for Research and Laboratory Management and initiated in February 2004.

The purpose of this study was to identify all potential users of high-performance computing (HPC) within the Army science and technology community and any barriers to full use of current and planned HPC resources. A main study goal was to help develop an Army HPC strategy and build an HPC initiative that facilitates that strategy, thereby allowing the Army to compete effectively for Department of Defense HPC resources and to ensure that they are used for maximum effect in attacking the most difficult and computationally intensive research problems critical to future force and future combat systems achievement. This research was sponsored by the Director for Research and Laboratory Management of the Office of the Assistant Secretary of the Army for Acquisition, Logistics and Technology.

This report is tailored to the Army's Director for Research and Laboratory Management. As such, it assumes knowledge of Army plans for transformation and development of a future force and key research and development (R&D) requirements stemming from these plans.

This research was conducted in RAND Arroyo Center's Force Development and Technology Program. RAND Arroyo Center, part of the RAND Corporation, is a federally funded research and development center sponsored by the United States Army. Questions and comments regarding this research are welcome and should be directed to the leader of the research team, Dr. Robert H. Anderson, at anderson@rand.org.

For more information on RAND Arroyo Center, contact the Director of Operations (telephone 310-393-0411, extension 6419; FAX 310-451-6952; email Marcy_Agmon@ rand.org), or visit Arroyo's web site at http://www.rand.org/ard/.

Contents

Preface iii

Figures vii

Tables ix

Summary xi

Acknowledgments xv

Abbreviations xvii

CHAPTER ONE

Introduction 1

CHAPTER TWO

HPC: What Is It? Where Is It Going? 3

HPC Today 3

    Cluster Examples 4

    Grid Examples 4

HPC Futures 5

    Microprocessor Design 6

    Interconnect Technologies 6

    Memory 6

    I/O and Storage 6

    Packaging 6

    Reliability, Availability, Serviceability (RAS) 7

    The Future Depends on the Funding 7

    U.S. Government HPC Initiatives 7

CHAPTER THREE

Overview of Current HPC Use Within Army R&D 9

Workshop Results 9

    HPC Software 10

    Resource Availability and Allocation 10

    HPC as an Enabler and a Predictor 11

Challenges Identified at the Workshop 11

Biotechnology and Biomedical Army R&D HPC Applications 12

C2 Battlefield Networking 13

CHAPTER FOUR

A Focus on Biotech/Biomed Applications 15

The Importance of Biotechnology 15

How Can HPC Benefit Biotechnology Research? 16

    Bioinformatics 16

    Systems Biology 17

    Computational Physiology 17

    Molecular Modeling 17

The Need for HPC in Biotechnology Research 17

Army R&D and Biotech/Biomed Research 18

    Design of Biological Sentinels 18

    Theater Genomic Database for Early Warning and Detection of Biological Threats 19

    Design of Vaccines and Immune Enhancement for Ad Hoc Threats 20

    Modeling for Wound Healing, Casualty Treatment, and Performance Enhancement 21

    Biomimicry and Mob Psychology 21

    Quick-Response Terrorism Modeling Tool Set 22

    Development and Exploitation of Powerful Visualization Tools 22

    Current Status of Opportunities 23

CHAPTER FIVE

A Focus on C4ISR Network Modeling and Simulation 25

CHAPTER SIX

Common Tools and Techniques Across Bio and Network Application Areas 33

CHAPTER SEVEN

Findings 43

CHAPTER EIGHT

Recommendations 45

Appendix: November 17, 2004, Army R&D HPC Workshop 47

Bibliography 51

Figures

3.1. HPC Projects and Resource Use 10

3.2. Army HPCMP 2004 Projects by CTA 12

5.1. State of the Art of C2 Network Modeling/Simulation 26

5.2. CERDEC C4ISR Effects M&S Process 27

5.3. Links and Platforms of Future Communications Architectures 28

5.4. Effect of Vertical Nodes on Communication Throughput 28

5.5. Tradeoff Between Robustness and Efficiency 29

5.6. Example of Qualnet Simulation Experiment 30

5.7. Effect of UAVs on Network Performance 30

5.8. Screen Shot from Urban Resolve 31

6.1. Hierarchical Modeling of Structures and Systems 34

6.2. Metabolic Pathways 36

6.3. Gene Regulatory Network for the Sea Urchin 38

6.4. Cases of Node Connectivity 39

6.5. P(k) for E. Coli 40

Tables

2.1. Hardware Roadmap: No Future R&D Support (Current Program) 7

2.2. Hardware Roadmap: Robust R&D Plan 8

2.3. U.S. Government HPC Initiatives and Sponsors 8

3.1. CHSSI Categories of HPC Application Areas 12

6.1. Parallels Between Bio and C2 Network Modeling Applications 40

Summary

Members of this project have studied the academic and industrial uses of HPC and have conducted site visits at a number of Army R&D HPC user and provider sites, including the Medical Research and Materiel Command (MRMC), Edgewood Chemical Biological Center (ECBC), the Army Research Lab's Major Shared Resource Center (MSRC), the Developmental Test Command (DTC), Research, Development, and Engineering Command's (RDECOM's) Communications-Electronics Research, Development, and Engineering (RD&E) Center (CERDEC), Scalable Network Technologies, Inc., and the Director for Command, Control, Communication, Computers, Intelligence, Surveillance, and Reconnaissance (C4ISR) for Future Combat Systems (FCS) at Boeing, Huntington Beach, California.

Because of the breadth of possible uses of HPC in Army R&D, our client asked us to concentrate on two HPC application areas: biotechnology and biomedicine, and modeling and simulation of the complex battlefield wireless network communication systems. We did so, and concluded that these areas are of great importance and merit focused funding and attention.

Our primary recommendations are these:

- Because both biotech and communications network modeling are important, we believe that incremental HPC R&D funding from the Assistant Secretary of the Army for Acquisition, Logistics, and Technology (ASA(ALT)) should concentrate on developing common tools and techniques valuable in both areas; we provide several examples of HPC tools of relevance to both areas.

- DoD challenge grants work effectively to focus attention and resources on new areas; ASA(ALT) should consider a small challenge grant program tailored to the unique needs of Army R&D.

- There are important uses for additional Army HPC "swat teams," which can provide training, startup aid, and links to High Performance Computing Modernization Office (HPCMO) software toolkits for new users and applications; this is especially needed with the proliferation of HPC to individual labs due to the availability of inexpensive personal computer (PC) clusters acting as supercomputers.

- ASA(ALT) should consider recommending the addition of a "BIO" computational technology area (CTA), and possibly one ("NET") tailored to communication network modeling and simulation, to focus attention on these important HPC applications.

In biotechnology/biomedicine, there are very important R&D application areas specific to Army needs, for example, rapid creation and tailoring of vaccines. The establishment in FY 2004 of a Biotechnology HPC Software Applications Institute at MRMC is an important first step, but many biological R&D topics of vital importance to the Army are not being addressed currently. Indeed, in our study of FY 2004 data, we found that only four of 115 HPC projects were of a biotech nature, and most of those related to dispersion or epidemiological modeling. A number of biotech/biomed applications are of vital interest to the Army but are not being given the attention they deserve.

In C4ISR modeling and simulation, CERDEC has very substantial expertise. It understands the problem well and it has in-house competence and focus on the problem. But battlefield network modeling does not scale well with increasing parallelization of computation, so the problem is currently intractable for analyzing tens of thousands of intercommunicating nodes in a battlefield scenario. Therefore, the Army's FCS is being designed without the benefit of such large-scale *detailed* analyses and simulations; simplifications are being made, of necessity, which may or may not prove realistic.

We find clusters of commercial off-the-shelf PCs (most often with high-speed backplanes) increasingly dominating HPC because of their cost-effectiveness. But vector machines do outperform cluster computing by a substantial amount and will continue to have an important role at the high (and expensive) end of HPC. There is a continuing tension as more R&D centers want to obtain in-house cluster computing to support their local HPC needs, yet that trend tends to scatter and distribute HPC software and operational expertise—perhaps below a critical mass at many locations. Meanwhile, the MSRCs wish to provide centralized HPC services to the Department of Defense (DoD) R&D community, which some users regard as too batch-oriented with delays and too uncertain in terms of security, not allowing them to build sufficient in-house expertise in all aspects of HPC use.

One question this study addressed was: "Is Army HPC R&D getting its fair share of DoD HPC resources?" The short answer is yes—although the Army has a smaller number of HPC projects using shared DoD resources, it gets about a third of the teraflops available.

Throughout this project, we were impressed by the operations and facilities of the DoD HPCMO, and its Common HPC Software Support Initiative (CHSSI) and Programming Environment and Training (PET) initiative. They seem well-respected in the DoD HPC community, although, of course more could be done in all of these areas as cluster computing brings HPC to many more sites and laboratories.

Because resources for new initiatives in Army HPC R&D are limited, we concentrated on describing some tools and techniques that appear to be common across both the biotech and network modeling application areas. These include better tools for multiresolution models that describe hierarchical structures and systems, application of network concepts for analysis of complex biological processes, and the use of some biological concepts within C2 network modeling.

Our primary recommendation is that the set of common tools and techniques spanning both the bio and network modeling application areas be given priority for funding. These include post-processing, visualization, hierarchical decomposition processes, and accelerators for processor-intensive activities such as line-of-sight calculations.

We are very impressed with the ability of the High Performance Computing Modernization Program (HPCMP) challenge grants to focus resources and attention on specific areas of DoD interest. ASA(ALT) might consider a smaller, even more focused program patterned after the HPCMP one, tailored to specific Army requirements.

We recommend that additional resources be provided to study the concept of an Army-specific HPC "swat team" that can focus on a particular laboratory's interests, provide specialized training and education in HPC, help migrate applications from serial to parallel computing architectures, and adapt and use the software tools and toolkits of the CHSSI program within the HPCMP. After several weeks or months of such intensive support, the team would leave a residual staff behind and tackle the next lab or agency in need of such focused assistance. Such a team should be supplemented by an HPC "help line" for those Army R&D organizations needing other HPC-related assistance. The purpose of this recommendation is to address the growing use of "home-grown" HPC within individual labs (e.g., using small- to medium-sized clusters) and the problem of having less-than-critical-mass expertise in HPC within those separate labs and agencies.

We believe ASA(ALT) should support the use of cluster computing for HPC within individual labs and agencies. These provide valuable hands-on HPC expertise and allow the migration, development, and debugging of HPC-related codes in a more interactive, intensive manner than submitting batch jobs to an MSRC.

A workshop we conducted in November 2004 highlighted what we have called "conceptual, tactical, and cultural problem areas" related to HPC use. End-users or customers of Army R&D have often asked, "Why is HPC needed for this?" "Will the resulting HPC-driven models and simulations replace any field testing?" "What is the business case for using HPC, as opposed to our normal methods?" Someone within the Army lab system should be tasked to compile "lessons learned" and accurate data and logic stating *when* HPC is best used, *how* it will affect outcomes, and *why* it is worthwhile in particular application areas. Analysis based on business cases should be provided to support these lessons learned. These questions are apparently encountered often enough that guidance and support for answering them are needed.

Last, we recommend that the Army request that the HPCMP add one or two CTAs to their existing list (or else recast some existing ones). The purpose is to give prominence and focus to the areas of biotech/biomed R&D and network modeling and simulation (with special attention to large-scale mobile communication networks). At present, these R&D application areas are scattered among a number of CTAs.

The above recommendations constitute a plan for focusing incremental Army R&D HPC activities, in addition to the substantial and important work already under way in more traditional areas such as computational fluid dynamics and projectile/armor impact studies.

Acknowledgments

We have received very substantial assistance on this project from all the agencies, centers, and individuals mentioned in this report as well as from our client, the Director for Laboratory Management, Office of the Assistant Secretary of the Army for Acquisition, Logistics, and Technology. We would like to thank many of our RAND colleagues, among them Thomas Herbert, Morgan Kisselburg, and Brad Wilson, for their recommendations and insights on high-performance computing. We received valuable reviewer comments from Ralph Roskies, Scientific Director of the Pittsburgh Supercomputer Center, and our RAND colleague Elliot Axelband. The findings and recommendations in this document are the authors', however, and do not necessarily represent those of the reviewers.

Abbreviations

AHPCRC	Army High Performance Computing Research Center
ASA(ALT)	Assistant Secretary of the Army for Acquisition, Logistics, and Technology
ARDEC	Armaments Research, Development, and Engineering Center
ARL	Army Research Laboratory
ARSC	Arctic Region Supercomputing Center
ASIC	Application Specific Integrated Circuit
ATC	Advanced Technology Centre
BIO	Biotechnology and Biomedicine
BIRN	Biomedical Informatics Research Network
C2	Command and Control
C4ISR	Command, Control, Communication, Computers, Intelligence, Surveillance, and Reconnaissance
CAA	Center for Army Analysis
CACR	Center for Advanced Computing Research (at CalTech)
CCM	Computational Chemistry and Materials Science
CEA	Computational Electromagnetics and Acoustics
CEN	Computational Electronics and Nanoelectronics
CERDEC	Communications-Electronics Research, Development, and Engineering Center
CFD	Computational Fluid Dynamics
CHSSI	Common High Performance Computing Software Support Initiative
CONUS	Continental United States
COTS	Commercial Off-the-Shelf
CPU	Computer Processing Unit
CSM	Computational Structural Mechanics

CTA	Computational Technology Area
CWA	Chemical Warfare Agent
CWO	Climate/Weather/Ocean Modeling and Simulation
DARPA	Defense Advanced Research Projects Agency
DNT	Dinitrotoluene
DoD	Department of Defense
DoE	Department of Energy
DREN	Defense Research Network
DTC	Developmental Test Command
ECBC	Edgewood Chemical Biological Center
EO	Electro-Optical
EQM	Environmental Quality Modeling and Simulation
ERDC	Engineering and Research Development Center
FCS	Future Combat Systems
FMS	Forces Modeling and Simulation
FPGA	Field Programmable Gate Array
FSL	Forecast System Laboratory
Gbit/sec	Gigabits per Second
GMO	Genetically Modified Organism
GPS	Global Positioning System
HEC	High-End Computing
HP	Hewlett-Packard
HPC	High Performance Computing
HPCC	High Performance Computing Centers
HPCMP	High Performance Computing Modernization Program
HPCMO	High Performance Computing Modernization Office
HPCS	High Productivity Computing System
IATAC	Information Assurance Technology Analysis Center
IED	Improvised Explosive Device
IMT	Integrated Modeling and Test Environments
I/O	Input/Output
IP	Internet Protocol
ITM	Irregular Terrain Model
JFCOM	Joint Forces Command

LED Light-Emitting Diode

M&S Modeling and Simulation

MPI Message Passing Interface

MRMC Army Medical Research and Materiel Command

MSRC Major Shared Resource Center

NBC Nuclear, Biological, and Chemical

NCSA National Center for Supercomputing Applications

NLR National LambdaRail

NMI National Science Foundation Middleware Initiative

NSF National Science Foundation

NVAC National Visual Analytics Center

ORNL Oak Ridge National Laboratory

PAIW Project Albert International Workshop

PC Personal Computer

PCR Polymerase Chain Reaction

PEO Program Executive Office

PET Programming Environment and Training (initiative of the HPCMP)

petaflops Thousand Teraflops

PIM Processor in Memory

PNNL Pacific Northwest National Laboratory

PSC Pittsburgh Supercomputing Center

QCD Quantum Chromodynamics

QCDoC Quantum Chromodynamics on a Chip

RAS Reliability, Availability, Serviceability

R&D Research and Development

RD&E Research, Development, and Engineering

RDECOM Research, Development, Engineering Command

RSTA Reconnaissance, Surveillance, and Target Acquisition

SAI Software Applications Institute

SDSC San Diego Supercomputer Center

SEAS System Effectiveness Analysis Simulation

SETA System Engineering and Technical Assistance

SETI Search for Extraterrestrial Intelligence

SIP	Signal/Image Processing
SMDC	Space and Missile Defense Command
TACC	Texas Advanced Computing Center
TACOM	Tank-Automotive and Armaments Command
TAM	Theater Agent-Based Modeling
TCP	Transmission Control Protocol
teraflops	Trillion Floating Point Operations per Second
TIC	Toxic Industrial Chemical
TIREM	Terrain-Integrated Rough Earth Model
TNT	Trinitrotoluene
UA	Unit of Action
UAV	Unmanned Aerial Vehicle
UDP	User Datagram Protocol
UE	Unit of Engagement
UGS	Unattended Ground Sensor
WSMR	White Sands Missile Range

CHAPTER ONE

Introduction

The Army's Director for Research and Laboratory Management asked RAND Arroyo Center to study the uses of and opportunities for high-performance computing (HPC) within Army research and development (R&D) labs and those of their associated contractors.

Our client asked us to concentrate on two areas: biotechnology (including biomedical applications) and modeling, simulation, and analysis of complex command and control (C2) wireless networks, comprising thousands or tens of thousands of mobile nodes, under battlefield conditions. Our approach to the research was, first, to find out what others were doing with HPC, particularly in academia and industry. We then determined what the Army was doing by surveying the allocation and use of HPC at Army-level agencies; laboratories within the Research, Development, and Engineering Command (RDECOM); and research and development centers.

Having reached preliminary conclusions, we held a workshop at RAND on Army R&D use of HPC in November 2004. Feedback and presentations received from that workshop have influenced the final conclusions and recommendations we present here.

The remainder of this report covers the following: a brief review of HPC and key trends in this field (Chapter Two); a discussion of current HPC usage within Army R&D (Chapter Three); biotechnology and biomedical application areas of promise, to which Army R&D might be focused (Chapter Four); command and control modeling, simulation, and analysis as an HPC application area (Chapter Five); and common tools and techniques for effective use of HPC that span a number of HPC application areas, including those highlighted in the two previous chapters (Chapter Six).

We conclude with some project findings (Chapter Seven) and our resulting recommendations for the Assistant Secretary of the Army for Acquisition, Logistics and Technology (ASA(ALT)) investments in HPC usage for Army R&D (Chapter Eight).

The appendix contains the agenda and list of participants in the workshop held on November 17, 2004.

CHAPTER TWO

HPC: What Is It? Where Is It Going?

Although there is clear consensus on the value of high-performance computing, opinions still diverge on exactly what is meant by the phrase. Douglass Post (2004) referred to HPC as "the use of large-scale computers to address and solve important technical problems." Others refer to HPC's application to projects so large and requiring so much computing power to solve, that they would be impossible for any one computer or person to solve in a reasonable amount of time. But most users of the terminology include additional considerations, such as memory, storage requirements, and required turnaround time.

Some researchers and practitioners associate HPC with the need for a supercomputer, a time-dependent term that refers to the class of the most powerful computer systems worldwide at the time of reference. In fact, a defining characteristic of HPC is that it requires the problem to be broken into parts that are solved in parallel, rather than only serially. That is, parallel or distributed computing techniques are applied to the solution of computationally intensive applications. In this report, we use the most inclusive definition: *High-performance computing is the set of algorithms, hardware, and software needed to solve problems that require the most powerful computer systems at the time of solution.* Included in this category are both large, single-purpose machines (often called supercomputers) as well as networks (clusters) of machines implementing distributed computing; the defining characteristics are speed and parallelism.

HPC Today

Top500 HPC performance is now dominated by nonvector platforms. The benchmark used by the Top500 site,[1] however, measures the speed of the processors and does not take into account interconnects and memory speed which, of course, affect the actual application performance.

Some reasons users cite for transitioning from vector machines are:

- Vectorizing scientific computational codes proves increasingly difficult
- Clusters are a fraction of the cost and are flexible (i.e., they scale up when budget allows and are reconfigurable).

---

[1] Online at http://www.top500.org.

However, recent orders and current collaborators with U.S.-made vector supercomputers include: German National High Performance Computing Centers (HPCC), Oak Ridge National Laboratory (ORNL), Korea Meteorological Administration, Government Micro Resources, Inc., Pittsburgh Supercomputing Center (PSC), U.S. Army Space and Missile Defense Command (SMDC), Army High Performance Computing Research Center (AHPCRC), Arctic Region Supercomputing Center (ARSC), Sandia National Laboratories, Boeing, and Warsaw University. Therefore, the market for specialized HPC hardware is far from exhausted.

In our study of current HPC applications (as of mid-2004), we uncovered the following examples of HPC clusters in use. We include also a list of "grid computing" architectures, although their more decentralized nature makes them marginal for all but the most relaxed, long-term applications (such as the Search for Extraterrestrial Intelligence (SETI)).

Cluster Examples

Tungsten

- At the National Center for Supercomputing Applications (NCSA), the HPCC's 1,400+ Dell PowerEdge™ servers with 15.3 teraflops peak via approximately 2,500 processors

Forecast System Laboratory (FSL) at the National Oceanic and Atmospheric Administration

- Dual Xeon 2.2 GHz — Myrinet2000 — Cluster — Intel 1536 processors with 3.3 teraflops max and 6.7 teraflops peak
- Capability for environmental modeling efforts that are carried out by FSL and non-FSL researchers

Grid Examples

Distributed computing over vast distances using specified resources appears to be emerging as a factor in HPC.

- **Teragrid:** nationally integrated system of supercomputing resources broadly accessible by scientists and engineers; more than 20 teraflops; applications include universe evolution, contaminated groundwater cleanup, simulating seismic events, and analysis of biomolecular dynamics
- **Information Society Technologies Crossgrid Tool:** aims to facilitate running applications over distributed computing environments and is currently used to help predict flooding across Europe; led by the Polish supercomputing institute Cyfronet, with 21 partners in 11 countries across Europe
- **Grid-enabling:** Hewlett-Packard (HP) Services and HP Labs, along with BAE SYSTEMS' Advanced Technology Centre (ATC), the Welsh e-Science Centre at Cardiff University, and the University of Wales, Swansea, preparing ATC concept design and test applications for the grid (e.g., More Electric Aircraft and the All Electric Ship)

- **Grid3**: National Science Foundation (NSF) and Department of Energy (DoE) collaboration for data-intensive elementary particle simulations via an international data grid spread across 28 sites in the United States and abroad, and the NSF Middleware Initiative (NMI)
- **University of North Carolina project**: aims to develop advanced research and education applications in high-performance computing, information systems, and computational and computer science; several universities are to collaborate and will include a focus on teaching undergraduates to use a computer grid to solve large computational problems
- **National LambdaRail (NLR)**: a privately funded network linking a dozen U.S. universities with four optical wavelengths, each operating at 10 gigabits per second (Gbit/sec); is viewed as a means to provide faculty access to supercomputing centers and other academic institutions
- **Biomedical Informatics Research Network (BIRN)**: includes 14 universities and 22 research groups; will support large-scale data sharing and analysis in health care research

HPC Futures

Several recent publications[2] give a fairly complete and accurate picture of future developments in the HPC hardware area. We drew heavily on these reports in producing this survey.

In general terms, we can expect continuing increases in the power of processing elements; Moore's Law looks as though it will continue for several more generations, although it is not clear that it will continue for another ten years. Memory bandwidth will improve, along with interconnect speeds, especially if sufficient funding is available for R&D in the HPC area. Increasing emphasis will be given to massively parallel architectures containing thousands of processors, provided the software tools for using such architectures are also developed.

Vector processing for certain high-end applications is also needed (e.g., cryptanalysis and quantum molecular modeling). Since there is no large-scale need for such processors, these will be developed only for the HPC market and only in small quantities. However, we expect such machines to be built in multiprocessor configurations but not with the large number of processors found in conventional parallel machines.

Within ten years, systems capable of ten petaflops performance should appear. With sufficient funding, performance in the hundred petaflops range should be possible.

In specific terms, five areas influence the future development of HPC hardware, namely, microprocessor design, interconnect technologies, memory, input/output (I/O), storage, and packaging. As the *Federal Plan for High-End Computing* explains, the scale of this development will depend critically on the amount of federal R&D funding made available for HPC hardware design.

The possible developments for each of these areas are described briefly in the following sections.

---

[2] *Federal Plan for High-End Computing* (2004); Computing Research Association (2003).

Microprocessor Design

It is expected that microprocessors with 1.5 billion transistors will be introduced by 2010, a fivefold increase over today's production systems. However, performance will be optimized to serve the high-volume commercial market. HPC requires different chip architectures and subsystems for optimal performance. For example, the use of multiple computer processing unit (CPU) cores per chip will be accompanied by a decrease in the memory bandwidth per CPU, which is not optimal for many HPC calculations. On the other hand, opportunities exist for the development of nontraditional processors based on FPGAs (field programmable gate arrays), PIMs (processors in memory), or ASICs (application specific integrated circuits) with licensed information processing cores (such as IBM is using in the Quantum Chromo-dynamics on a Chip (QCDoC) machine being built for QCD (quantum chromodynamics) calculations. Such developments could lead to petaflop performance in the near future.

Interconnect Technologies

One of the biggest bottlenecks in modern computers from the point of view of HPC calculations is the relatively poor match of the communication latency of these machines to their processor performance. Such latency and bandwidth limits must be improved across the whole range of interconnects within a system. With appropriate funding, optical interconnects could be developed with orders of magnitude more bandwidth than current systems.

Memory

Although processor speed has followed Moore's Law and steadily increased every year for some time now, memory latency and bandwidth has increased far more slowly (at approximately 7 percent per year). As a result, HPC applications can never achieve the full performance level of the processors available, since the processors must often wait for the data required for the calculation. Increasing integration of memories in the processors, or the use of PIMs, can improve this situation, as well as the development of coupled high-bandwidth memory and processor systems tailored to HPC applications. However, the most effective memory structure, in particular, shared versus distributed memory, will depend on the class of problems being solved, and the choice made will have a large effect on the overall cost of the system. Significant investment is needed to foster the development of appropriate memory technologies for HPC applications.

I/O and Storage

Terascale and petascale HPC applications in the future will generate and use massive amounts of data that must be stored and managed. Current developments are producing significant increases in storage capacity, but latency and bandwidth improvements occur much more slowly.

Packaging

The requirements for integration in future computer components will mandate increasing emphasis on heat dissipation and power consumption, among other things. Although these are not directly connected to the performance of a system, they must be considered in any given system design. Thermal management of future HPC systems will require R&D for new liquid, air, and cryogenic cooling technologies beyond those the market will produce on its own.

Reliability, Availability, Serviceability (RAS)

As more and more machines or processors are connected into a single system, the ability of the system to continue operating after the failure of any component, and to undergo maintenance without shutting down the whole system, becomes increasingly important. HPC manufacturers are putting considerable resources into solving this problem.

The Future Depends on the Funding

The *Federal Plan for High-End Computing* summarizes nicely the future of HPC hardware in the two cases in which no future R&D support occurs and a robust R&D plan is funded. These cases are summarized in Tables 2.1 and 2.2. Presumably, the final outcome will lie somewhere in between.

Overall, we find that high-performance computing is increasingly dominated by clusters of commodity PCs, wired together with fast "backplane" networks allowing exchange of data among the computational nodes in the cluster. Clusters of 64, 128, and 256 are common, with 2,048 becoming available when needed. (However, Lawrence Livermore National Laboratory intends to purchase an IBM BlueGene/L machine in 2005 capable of a theoretical 360 teraflops, containing 131,072 processors.) Vector machines continue to be highly desirable for specialized applications, as mentioned above, but with the considerably lower expense of "off-the-shelf" PC clusters, the trend toward their increasing use is clear. This has implications for the centralized Department of Defense (DoD) Major Shared Resource Centers (MSRCs), as will be discussed below.

U.S. Government HPC Initiatives

The future of HPC will also be affected by a number of U.S. government initiatives promoting HPC with the explicit aim of regaining a U.S. lead in supercomputing. Several key initiatives are listed in Table 2.3.

Table 2.1
Hardware Roadmap: No Future R&D Support (Current Program)

	Near-Term	Mid-Term	Long-Term
Microarchitecture	COTS-driven microarchitecture	Multi-CPU cores per chip, memory bandwidth per CPU decreases	Moore's Law ends?
Interconnect technologies	Interconnect technology based on electrical interconnect and electrical switches	Interconnect technology based on electro-optical interconnect and electrical switches	Interconnect technology driven by telecom—expect moderate advances for HEC systems
Memory	Processor/memory performance gap addressed by caches, limits performance and ease of programming	Early COTS PIM-based and streaming technologies to address processor/memory gap	Evolutionary improvements; increased use of PIMs
Power, cooling, and packaging	Thermal packaging—chip/system technologies limited by the ability to air-cool	Evolutionary improvements do not significantly advance our ability to develop high-end systems	System performance limited by thermal effects?
I/O and storage	I/O driven by COTS-based needs in areas of storage and links	Petaflop-scale file systems based on COTS technologies, RAS issues will limit usability	Depends on 3D storage

NOTE: COTS = commercial off-the-shelf; HEC = high-end computing.

Table 2.2
Hardware Roadmap: Robust R&D Plan

	Near- to Mid-Term	Long-Term
Microarchitecture	Prototype microprocessors developed for HEC systems available	Innovative post-silicon technology optimized for HEC
Interconnect technologies	Interconnect technology based on optical interconnect and electrical switches	All-optical interconnect technology for HEC
Memory	Memory systems developed for HEC needs; accelerated introduction of PIMs	Revolutionary high-bandwidth memory at petaflop scale
Power, cooling, and packaging	Stacked 3D memory and advanced cooling technologies address critical design limitations	Ability to address high-density packaging throughout the entire system
I/O and storage	Petaflop-scale file systems with RAS focused on HEC requirements	Revolutionary approaches to exascale "file systems"

Table 2.3
U.S. Government HPC Initiatives and Sponsors

Participants	Activity
Several teams—University of Delaware, IBM, Massachusetts Institute of Technology, Cornell University, University of Illinois at Champaign-Urbana, University of California at Berkeley, and the University of Texas at Austin; Cray and New Technology Endeavors; and Sun Microsystems	High Productivity Computing Systems (HPCS) initiative to regain preeminence in supercomputing
Argonne National Laboratory, Center for Advanced Computing Research (CACR) at CalTech, Indiana University, NCSA, ORNL, PSC, Purdue University, San Diego Supercomputer Center (SDSC), Texas Advanced Computing Center (TACC) at the University of Texas at Austin	Teragrid: widely shared supercomputing infrastructure
Approximately 65 academic institutions and the ten DoE Office of Science laboratories; 2,400+ scientists in universities, federal agencies, and U.S. companies	Advanced Scientific Computing Research program funds high-performance supercomputing, networking, and software development (recent award to build a 50 teraflop science research computer for national competitiveness)
Department of Energy's Pacific Northwest National Laboratory (PNNL)	National Visual Analytics Center (NVAC) research and development of tools and methods for managing, visualizing, and analyzing enormous amounts of diverse data and information

Overview of Current HPC Use Within Army R&D

Our survey of HPC use within Army R&D labs and RDECOM relied heavily on yearly survey data (in our case, for FY 2004) obtained by the DoD High Performance Computing Modernization Office (HPCMO). We obtained from HPCMO a database "slice" of all Army data for FY 2004. We also conducted site visits to a number of labs and installations, including Medical Research and Materiel Command (MRMC); Edgewood Chemical Biological Center (ECBC); the Army Research Lab's MSRC; the Developmental Test Command (DTC); RDECOM's Communications-Electronics Research, Development, and Engineering Center (CERDEC); Scalable Network Technologies, Inc.; and the Director for Command, Control, Communication, Computers, Intelligence, Surveillance, and Reconnaissance (C4ISR) for Future Combat Systems (FCS) at Boeing, Huntington Beach, California.

One question we were investigating was: "Is the Army getting its 'fair share' of DoD HPC resources?" The short answer is "yes." Although the *number* (115) of Army *projects* is less than those of the Navy and Air Force, in terms of HPC resource utilization, the Army receives about one-third of all HPCMO-provided computational power.

Figure 3.1 shows how the Army compares to other services in its participation in the High Performance Computing Modernization Program (HPCMP) and in its usage of computing resources. It seems at first glance that the Army does not participate at the same level as other services, when looking at the number of projects. However, during the November workshop, we learned that some Army-level agencies, such as the Army Research Laboratory (ARL) and the Enginering and Research Development Center (ERDC), combine individual projects into larger ones to control administrative costs and burdens . Further, a better indicator of use and participation is resource utilization. In this regard, the Army is on par with other services.

Workshop Results

Part of our assessment of the current state of HPC usage within Army R&D included conducting a workshop in November 2004 at RAND's offices in Arlington, Virginia. Some findings resulting from that workshop follow.

Figure 3.1
HPC Projects and Resource Use

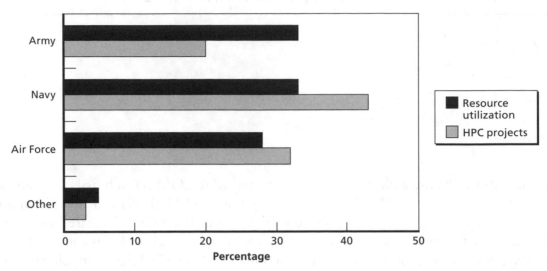

SOURCE: Compiled from data provided by High Performance Computing Modernization Office (2004).
RAND *TR310-3.1*

HPC Software

Most HPC applications use the Message Passing Interface (MPI) software for interprocess communication, except when great efficiency is required. The HPCMO Common High Performance Computing Software Support Initiative (CHSSI) program is developing a "toolkit" of very useful software for HPC programmers and end-users.

We note that there is considerable HPC activity under way in cluster computing involving four to 64 or so CPUs, where some parallelism is exploited. There is also much use of highly parallel vector machines for specialized computations. As cluster computing with "blades" becomes less expensive and backplanes linking the CPUs together become faster, there will be increasing emphasis on clusters involving 64 to 128 to 256 and more CPUs—and the migration of software to these architectures will absorb much time and other resources. Software to ease the graceful migration of an application among such clusters will be in great demand.

Resource Availability and Allocation

The MSRCs provide a valuable source of computation and expertise in HPC. They have a variety of both vector and cluster-computing architectures available for use locally or via high-speed access from the Defense Research Network (DREN). However, some tension exists between shared resource centers and local HPC facilities. Many Army labs wish to have local control of cluster computers for experimentation, for use in migration of applications to cluster HPCs, for test and evaluation, and for limited test runs. Some sites also want local control when running classified applications. (After these activities, the applications—if very computationally intensive—would presumably migrate to the MSRCs for "final" runs.)[1]

_____

[1] One of our interviewees made the point that the MSRCs should concentrate on the very largest, most intensive HPC jobs and should ensure that their scheduling algorithms favored such jobs even if that resulted in "utilization" figures that were less than optimal.

Some sites want to acquire cluster computing as a way of developing in-house competence. Users also increasingly want interactive, "hands-on" access during their program's execution, to visualize whether the computation is on track and producing interesting results.

All these pressures toward local computation (performed in addition to those in the MSRCs) will result in a greater need for decentralized training and expertise. The HPCMO Programming Environment and Training (PET) initiative is very relevant in this regard and provides very valuable services. We feel that Army R&D may need to supplement the PET activities with additional training, particularly in migrating existing applications to HPC parallelism of various types.

HPC as an Enabler and a Predictor

At the November workshop, there was discussion of HPC as *enabling* a variety of applications vital to the Army and its R&D program. Key areas include Army transformation; systems engineering and analysis of C4ISR architectures; design, test, and evaluation for survivability and lethality techniques; R&D for force health protection; immersive visualization techniques; sensor technology for detecting unexploded ordnance, improvised explosive devices (IEDs), and mines; and cyber security.

Another role of HPC is to help *predict* a variety of futures, such as atmospheric conditions or how various blast and projectile effects will interact with differing structures. Some of these predictive applications will increasingly be operational, with HPC models and simulations tapped into from the battlefield for planning and allocation purposes. It will be increasingly important for the Army to consider migrating results from its HPC-related R&D program into operational code that is available to warfighters via networks directly on the battlefield.

Challenges Identified at the Workshop

At the November workshop, various challenges to the use of HPC in Army R&D were discussed. The conceptual challenge is from "customers" of Army research who ask about capabilities and have little interest in how those capabilities are provided—by HPC or by other computational or design/test means. HPC researchers are being asked to develop a business case regarding why HPC resources are needed to solve a customer's problem.

Other challenges include having tools to help decide what the appropriate computing architecture for a problem is and what "menu" of batch, interactive, and other computational runs will best lead to a solution to the problem at hand. Finally, there was discussion of the need for greater awareness and training throughout Army R&D in the abilities of HPC to provide unique approaches to the hardest modeling and simulation problems.

We next turned our attention to the *content* of the Army HPC projects listed in the HPCMO database. Figure 3.2 shows the breakdown of projects by computational technology area (CTA). DoD's HPCMP's CHSSI categorizes projects within one or more of 10 CTAs; the CTAs used by CHSSI are listed in Table 3.1.

Figure 3.2 shows the projects as a percentage of the whole by area. Half of the projects by number fall into two areas: computational fluid dynamics and computational structural dynamics.

Table 3.1
CHSSI Categories of HPC Application Areas

CSM	Computational Structural Mechanics
CFD	Computational Fluid Dynamics
CCM	Computational Chemistry and Materials Science
CEA	Computational Electromagnetics and Acoustics
CWO	Climate/Weather/Ocean Modeling and Simulation
SIP	Signal/Image Processing
FMS	Forces Modeling and Simulation/C4I
EQM	Environmental Quality Modeling and Simulation
CEN	Computational Electronics and Nanoelectronics
IMT	Integrated Modeling and Test Environments

Figure 3.2
Army HPCMP 2004 Projects by CTA

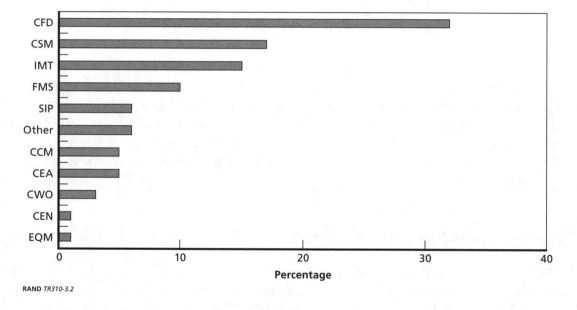

RAND *TR310-3.2*

Biotechnology and Biomedical Army R&D HPC Applications

Given our project's focus on biotech/biomed as one of two application areas of special interest, we note in Table 3.1 that there is no "BIO" CTA, which alone might bias some thinking about appropriate military uses of HPC away from biotech/biomed applications. And if such uses did exist, they could be scattered among several CTA areas, without focus or coordination.

We identified four of the 115 FY 2004 HPCMP projects that fit within the areas of biotech/biomed. These include three in the category of biological and chemical agent dispersal and one in contaminants and the ecosystem.

The Army Research Lab at Aberdeen Proving Ground, Maryland, is conducting a study called "Modeling and Simulations for Improved C4ISR Capabilities." The project is characterized as primarily a CFD problem, but also contains elements related to CCM, SIP, and FMS. The objective is to understand how nuclear, biological, and chemical (NBC) agents flow through extended urban areas by simulating the physics of the atmosphere carrying NBC agents. The goal is to improve C4ISR by integrating such a capability to improve situational awareness.

The ERDC at Vicksburg, Mississippi, is conducting a study called "Numerical Simulation of Contaminant Dispersion Within a Room Under a Typical HVAC System Operation." The project is characterized as a CFD problem and the goal is to simulate dispersion of chemical and biological contaminants.

TACOM is the Tank-Automotive and Armaments Command. The Army Armaments Research, Development, and Engineering Center (ARDEC) at Picatinny Arsenal, New Jersey, has a project called "The Imaging Analysis and Simulation." The project is characterized as a SIP problem and the objective is to profile the experimental results of detecting, monitoring, and identifying concealed chemical/biological agents via simulated continuous wave terahertz imaging spectroscopy.

ERDC, also at Vicksburg, has a project called "Environmental Quality." The project is characterized as primarily an EQM problem, but it also contains elements related to CCM and FMS. The objective is to develop a description and coding of the fate/transport of contaminants and other constituents through the ecosystem to include interconnections with multiple biological species in the aquatic and terrestrial environment.

We note that none of the projects listed above helps with the difficult modeling and engineering efforts at the molecular level that are relevant for Army applications.

C2 Battlefield Networking

We identified five of 115 FY 2004 HPCMP projects that fit within the area of networking. C2 wireless network modeling on a dynamic battlefield (our other application of special interest) is scattered among several CTA categories, as will be seen below.

ERDC at Vicksburg has a project called "3D Seismic/Acoustic Signature Simulation for Unattended Ground Sensor Networks." The project is characterized as primarily a CFD problem, but it also includes areas of CCM. The objective is to observe seismic and acoustic wave propagations and create target signature simulations from unattended ground sensor (UGS) systems and UGS systems networks.

The White Sands Missile Range (WSMR) in New Mexico has a project called "Range Operations Real-Time Test Display System." The project is characterized as an IMT problem. The goal is to develop a real-time display of mission progress and events using correlated telemetry, optics, radar, and global positioning system (GPS) data for project and test support personnel.

ATC at Aberdeen Proving Ground, Maryland, has two projects, both characterized as IMT problems. The first is called "Versatile Information System—Integrated, On-Line, Nationwide (VISION)" and is characterized as an IMT problem. The goal is to demonstrate that an information collection, dissemination, and management capability can be dispersed throughout a system (or system of systems) to collect and fuse greater quantities of data while camouflaging the complexity of the information infrastructure from users. The second project is called "Real Time Data Warehousing, On Line Analytical." The goal is to develop a lifecycle information management capability to intelligently and automatically assist in time-data fusion, knowledge extraction, and analytical processing of test data from modern weapon megasystems.

The Center for Army Analysis (CAA) at Fort Belvoir, Virginia, is conducting a study called "Theater Agent-Based Modeling (TAM)." The project is characterized as an FMS problem. This effort seeks to aggregate agent objects (every soldier and every piece of weaponry, sensors, and organization) to achieve an acceptable run-time for a theater-level combat model.

The Marine Corps Combat Development Warfighting Laboratory hosts workshops twice a year in which high-performance computing is used to "data-farm," i.e., run tens of thousands of simulations to create a set of data for analysis. This series of workshops is called the Project Albert International Workshop (PAIW). The focus tends to be on agent-based force-on-force simulators of various types including one called MANA. The Maui High Performance Computing Center and a cluster in Singapore are utilized for these activities.

Note that these few network-related modeling projects are scattered among the CTAs of CCM, CFD, FMS, and IMT.

Given this overview of Army R&D HPC usage, in the next two chapters we "drill down" in more detail into the two application areas we focused on: biotech/biomed, and command and control modeling and simulation related to tens of thousands of mobile nodes active in a battlefield environment.

CHAPTER FOUR

A Focus on Biotech/Biomed Applications

We were asked to consider whether Army R&D HPC applications should include a focus on biotechnology and biomedical studies.

The Importance of Biotechnology

It is clear that biotechnology is a vital R&D area for the Army. Among its direct applications of interest (listed in Defense Technical Information Center, 2003) are:

- *Medicine*: Vaccines for chem/bio threats; pharmaceuticals to combat infectious diseases and other threats; human performance enhancers
- *Biomarkers*: Quicker identification of soldiers' ailments; means to detect soldiers' genetic susceptibility to toxins and disease
- *Improved display and control*: Better understanding of molecular interactions, e.g., among drugs, between a virus and a protein, etc.; better display of systemic functions, e.g., soldiers' bodily organs.

Biotechnology is also vital to improve the quality of, and to expedite, medical treatment in the field, with access as necessary to remote computational facilities via high-performance networking. This topic will be discussed below.

Another recent report[1] had as its purpose "to examine the potential of biotechnology to revolutionize U.S. military capabilities and the readiness of DoD." Among the questions it asked were: "Which areas of biotechnology are most relevant to national security?" Among its findings are the statements:

> With few exceptions, DoD elements were focused on bio-defense, medical remediation or counter-proliferation. In our judgment, there appears to be an institutional DoD bias where biotechnology is still considered an "evil"—something which should be defended against, or whose proliferation should be countered. But, there is a small and growing community which views biotechnology as a new and potentially revolutionary science that should be embraced and applied to a broad range of military problems. Their work, however, is stunted by inadequate institutional, policy, and funding support . . .

---

[1] Information Assurance Technology Analysis Center (IATAC) (2002).

DoD plays a minor role in United States Government (USG) biotechnology R&D investment. DoD is only contributing 3.2 percent ($580 million) of the U.S. Government expenditures for biotechnology (FY '00 figures). Of the $580 million, over half ($296 million) is in medical and allied defense research. Less than 1.5 percent of USG biotech R&D is applied against non-traditional biotech applications.[2]

Appendixes C–E of that report contain "advanced exemplars" to illustrate what might become available to a future combat force:

- Advanced vaccines and immune enhancements for expeditionary warfare and homeland security (including gene vaccines, edible vaccines, and radioprotective nutraceuticals)
- Accelerated wound healing using light-emitting diodes (LEDs) and regeneration technologies
- Stasis for critical warfighter casualties
- Human performance enhancement exemplars
- Enhanced environmental endurance for the warfighter
- Enhanced cognition for improved warfighter performance
- Enhanced battlefield information processing through biocomputation
- Biology-based battlefield power supplies.

In general, the IATAC report is a powerful statement regarding the importance of long-range, sustained military funding of specialized biotechnology and biomedicine research. We have been informed by its author that the report is being updated, and a revision should be available in 2005.

How Can HPC Benefit Biotechnology Research?

High-performance computing is especially important in four areas of biotechnology research: bioinformatics, systems biology, computational physiology, and molecular modeling. We discuss each in turn.

Bioinformatics

Bioinformatics is the use of statistical data to perform genomic and proteomic analysis. Recent progress in this area includes the mapping of genomes of humans, the mustard plant, rice, and the fruit fly.

One main mystery yet to be unraveled regards proteins, which are synthesized from genes. Among the many unanswered questions pertaining to proteins we cite here just a few:

- What are the functions of different proteins?
- How long do they last, and when are they "turned off"?
- For gene modification purposes, what modifications will in turn cause what changes in protein function?

---

[2] Information Assurance Technology Analysis Center (2002, p. 13).

Systems Biology

Systems biology involves the dynamic description of cellular processes, which in turn helps in understanding diseases at the cellular level. Systems biology also involves the efforts toward integrating the vast amounts of accumulated biological knowledge (intracellular transport; cellular organelles; organs; pathology; circulatory, nervous, and immune systems; metabolic and other biochemical pathways; genomic, proteomic, physiologic and environmental data on multiple organisms, etc.) while at the same time adding the ability to explain how living beings work as complete systems. Furthermore, as its name suggests, it attempts to apply systems concepts to the study of biological problems.

The approach to systems biology is primarily mathematical and often uses extensive computer modeling. As an example, one creates a model of interactions of cells with viruses, bacteria, and other harmful microorganisms. Some of these models make use of long sequences of ordinary and partial differential equations.

Computational Physiology

Computational physiology is systems biology on a larger scale, modeling an entire organism, such as a human. Example applications are:

- Modeling dynamical systems that control heartbeats
- Explaining neuron firings in the brain (perhaps using analogies to chaos theory)
- Detecting and understanding system-level pathologies.

Closely related to computational physiology is bioengineering, which consists of the application of engineering principles to the fields of biology and medicine (e.g., in the development of aids or replacements for defective or missing body organs). It includes the engineering (design, fabrication, and testing) of genetically modified organisms (GMOs).

Molecular Modeling

Molecular modeling is the study of biomolecules (e.g., proteins, DNA, RHA, water) as little machines. Scientists seek to understand how such molecules interact with their environments. Numerous forces act on each molecule, such as electrostatic, Van der Waals covalent, and ionic forces—and molecules react to the actions surrounding molecules. The entire system must be modeled to understand, for example, how various molecular components (e.g., statins) will link and bond with other, more complex molecules, perhaps thereby blocking their activity.

The Need for HPC in Biotechnology Research

Three key uses for HPC use in biotechnology research stem from the need to

- Create movies/simulations of biological processes. Movies are a basic tool of computational biology, because they permit the user to visualize a biological system's behavior. The characteristic times of protein phenomena—such as protein folding—range from femtoseconds[3] to microseconds. And many biological processes take much longer than a microsecond.

- Model interactions of 10,000 to 100,000 molecules at a time. This is necessary to calculate the forces that characterize the many possible interactions, which is impossible to perform with just one processor in any reasonable time.
- Solve large systems of simultaneous ordinary or partial differential equations. Coefficients are not known and so must be guessed from an enormous parameter space. Highly parallel processing can help this process by expediting the evaluation of a wide range of such parameter values.

Army R&D and Biotech/Biomed Research

As was seen in the previous chapter, there are currently few biotech/biomed studies under way within the Army R&D portfolio. However, in FY 2004, a new "Biotechnology HPC Software Applications Institute (SAI)" was formed as part of an HPCMO competition. It is located at the U.S. Army MRMC, Ft. Detrick, Maryland, and is headed by Dr. Jaques Reifman. We visited Dr. Reifman at MRMC in May 2004. He also made a presentation on this new initiative at our November 2004 HPC workshop.

The new Bio HPC SAI is an important step forward in increasing the focus within Army R&D on bio applications. But its three initial focus areas for this institute are only a small subset of important bio applications vital to Army interests. They are as follows:

- Tools for identification of genomic/protemoic biomarkers
- Computational prediction of protein structure/function to support the development of medical countermeasures
- Biomolecular network modeling and simulation.

We believe that seven other areas of bio applications in three categories are vital (*preparatory*, i.e., relevant before battlefield operational usage; *reactive*, operational applications used in reaction to conditions found; and *tool sets*, general capabilities needed for bio-related modeling, simulation, and analysis).

We discuss these seven application areas in more detail.

Design of Biological Sentinels

The biological sentinel is a recently proposed concept that will allow living organisms, such as bacteria or plants, to detect or identify the presence of specific chemical threats, such as sarin, mustard gas, TNT (trinitrotoluene) and DNT (dinitrotoluene).[4] The concept is based on the manipulation/engineering of naturally occurring genetic circuits—such as the so-called "signal transduction pathways" and "signaling pathways." In an operational or tactical context, we can think of deploying engineered seeds of the target plant organism by aerial platforms, or even by special operation forces, well before the appearance of the threat. The plants would grow in this denied or politically sensitive territory. The plants' modified ge-

---

[3] A femtosecond is 10^{-15} seconds, a millionth of a nanosecond.

[4] For more on this topic, see Ferber (2004); Gerchman and Weiss (2004); Bobayashi et al. (2004); and Looger et al. (2003).

netic circuit would then be triggered by the presence of the specific chemical threat, and radiation emitted by fluorophores or quantum dots could be detected by a friendly observation platform. Thus, these "plant sentinels" would provide visual warning to, say, an airborne observation platform, revealing whether a declared enemy, a potential enemy, or a terrorist group is developing specific threats.

Work to this date has focused on manipulating the genetic circuits of a bacterium—such as the ubiquitous E. Coli. However, at least the intention exists to extend this research to more complicated "eukaryotic"[5] genetic circuits such as those of plants.

Design of biological sentinels involves the following steps. First, a genetic circuit in a target organism is identified. Such a circuit must include a receptor protein able to trigger activation of the circuit when binding to a specific extracellular molecule called a "ligand"—a ligand can be a molecule that the cell uses to survive, such as ribose, glucose, or another simple sugar.

Second, the receptor protein is engineered to become a molecular sensor able to bind to the target chemical threat instead of to its ligand. The starting point for this second step is the experimentally determined 3D structure of the naturally occurring receptor protein. The protein's ligand binding site is redesigned to recognize and bind to the chemical threat. The result is a modified 3D structure for the receptor protein, which turns it into a molecular sensor for the chemical threat. Last, an amino acid sequence able to yield the desired 3D structure is determined by "inverse protein folding."

The third step in the design of the biological sentinel consists of modifying the relevant genes, namely, the ones that will be activated (expressed) by the signal transduction pathway, so that, for example, a quantum dot or a "glowing protein"—such as a fluorophore—is generated after these genes are transcribed and translated.

Most of these steps are very computationally intensive. Thus, great benefit in computational speediness would result if they were performed within an HPC environment. Moreover, the challenge of designing biological sentinels will imply multidisciplinary approaches, which will benefit from techniques already implemented in genomic and proteomic research, genetic engineering, electrical engineering—control theory, in particular—and modeling and simulation of the environmental effects of sensors.

Theater Genomic Database for Early Warning and Detection of Biological Threats

A successful response to a biological attack on U.S. troops has to start with rapid, highly sensitive detection and identification of the pathogen or pathogens used by the enemy. Most current methods for early-warning bio-monitoring implement DNA analysis.[6] Trace amounts of the pathogen's DNA are amplified—typically via the Polymerase Chain Reaction or PCR—from a large pool of DNA taken from a theater's environmental sample. Specificity to a particular bioagent is accomplished by using so-called "DNA primers," short sequences of DNA that can only be base-paired to selected segments of the pathogen's DNA. Combining multiple primers permits screening of several pathogens' DNA. These techniques require a priori knowledge of the bioagent's genome in addition to PCR. Moreover, they ana-

---

[5] A eukaryotic cell has its genome enclosed inside a compartment called the cell nucleus, whereas a prokaryotic cell—like a bacterium—does not have such a compartment. There are other differences between the two types of cells. Multicellular organisms such as plants, animals, and humans are eukaryotes.

[6] See also Zimmerman, Swenson, and Golden (2004).

lyze only specific regions of their genomes and thus may miss the opportunity to catch a genetically engineered bioweapon.

The theater genomic database method requires neither a priori knowledge of the bioagents' genome nor DNA amplification. The theater's environmental sample is analyzed so that all found DNA is "fingerprinted" or "barcoded." Instead of using pathogen-specific DNA primers, the method uses DNA tags able to base-pair with a common DNA sequence, which is randomly located within the pathogen's genome. The analysis results in a unique DNA barcode or fingerprint per pathogen. The barcodes are integrated within a theater genomic database.

In operational or tactical contexts, this method would be implemented as follows. DNA fingerprint profiles of samples taken from the theater are collected. Air from the local airport, or water from the local supply, may furnish the theater environmental samples. The analysis is then performed over several days and used to develop a DNA barcode profile characteristic of the theater. This profile can be used as a "baseline genomic profile" when, using experts' advice, the commander is satisfied that the profile does characterize the theater. Profiles periodically collected over subsequent days are compared against the baseline to assess whether bioagents have started to infiltrate the theater. Indeed, any profile change would indicate the presence of new DNA species, whose measured genome can be compared against the genomes of known threats.

Rapid generation of the baseline and of periodic DNA profiles would be greatly facilitated by HPC. Furthermore, sophisticated pattern recognition software running in HPC would expedite the matching of new DNA species with existing genomic databases to assess the potential danger. The method is expected to barcode a significant part of the genomes so that genetically engineered bioweapons could also be detected as changes in the barcode profile. The full system could be trained to automatically detect threats.

Implementing this method will require not only massive processing but also the secure transport of large amounts of information—the genomic profiles and databases—from theater to the HPC's location, the latter most likely in the Continental United States (CONUS). This problem may be partially alleviated by also implementing some decentralized processing, in which part of the analysis is performed in theater or within a nearby coalition country also possessing HPC capabilities.

Design of Vaccines and Immune Enhancement for Ad Hoc Threats

Once chemical or biological threats have been identified and characterized—using, for example, the methods previously discussed—the next step is to decide on a course of action to eliminate the threat. One obvious course of action is to rapidly implement in theater a vaccine or an immune enhancement against the threat. Currently, much research and development is being carried out in academia, the Armed Services' laboratories, and the pharmaceutical industry to design and fabricate biological counters to known bioagents. But, what if the enemy deploys in theater an unknown and lethal pathogen or genetically modified virus or bacterium? Most likely, the known biological countermethods will be ineffective against such ad hoc threats. Army HPC can be instrumental in developing biological measures to counter such threats, especially if Army HPC researchers use all the software tools developed in universities, service labs, and industry (prediction of 3D structure and folding of proteins, representation of cellular circuits and pathways, etc.).

Modeling for Wound Healing, Casualty Treatment, and Performance Enhancement

With HPC, sophisticated software tools could be developed and employed to model biological processes important to the warfighter.[7] A few examples are described below.

Soldier incapacitation in the battlefield could often be averted if mechanisms for rapid tissue regeneration became available. The physiological process of organisms with a high capacity for tissue regeneration—such as flatworms—could be modeled using HPC. Knowledge acquired from these studies can be applied to humans because of the strong homology between the flatworm and human genomes.

The design of compresses, bandages, splints, and goggles, which would, for example, accelerate regenerative healing, could also be integrated with the modeling of the relevant physiological processes.

The window of opportunity to save the lives of soldiers who are victims of serious battlefield injuries is often short—sometimes on the order of minutes. By using stasis, that is, by substantially decreasing the soldier's metabolic demand, it may be possible to expand this window of opportunity and save a life. A significant step toward accomplishing this goal is accurate modeling of the physiological processes present in organisms able to down-regulate their metabolism.

Research has shown that sleep deprivation is related to neurotransmitters that are not normally present in a rested human being. Modeling of the relevant brain circuits may lead to the development of therapeutic methods able to reset these circuits without sleeping, thus extending a soldier's alertness in the battlefield.

Finally, HPC can permit the design and fast exploitation of software tools that combine and integrate the above models with models for casualty treatment (evacuation, stabilization, and triage).

Biomimicry and Mob Psychology

Biomimicry (from bios, meaning "life," and mimesis, meaning "to imitate") is a design principle that seeks sustainable solutions to human problems by consulting and emulating nature's time-tested patterns and strategies.[8] Biomimicry thrives to take inspiration from, emulate, or adapt nature's designs or behaviors.

Numerous new materials and processes inspired by nature have been proposed. A few examples follow: navigation based on a combination of magnetism, the sun, stars, and sight; emulation of homing pigeons, pets, salmon, and monarch butterflies; nanometer-size rotary motors that follow the principles of bacterial flagella or ubiquitous enzymes such as ATPase—responsible for "translocating" protons across the mitochondrial membrane, a fundamental cellular process during respiration; hard, fracture-resistant coatings resembling abalone mussel nacre, a crystalline coating that self-assembles atop protein templates; adhesives that set underwater without primers or catalysts, inspired by blue mussel adhesive; and self-healing materials emulating a rhinoceros horn.

We discuss two possible biomimicry applications amenable to modeling within an HPC environment: camouflage and cooperating and aggregate behavior. Adequate camouflage is of paramount importance for both dismounted and mounted warfighters. It is well

---

[7] See, for example, Warner et al. (2002).

[8] From http://bfi.org/node/380 .

known that numerous animal species—insects, squids, etc.—use many different types of camouflage for their protection. Current efforts have been successful in modeling static camouflage but less successful when dealing with dynamic situations. Research on active motion camouflage could greatly benefit from HPC modeling and simulation support. Second, some animals work in groups to confuse a predator and protect their offspring. Such animal cooperative and aggregate behavior, known as "mobbing" or "swarming," can be emulated by the Army to gain advantage over an adversary or to take control over a civilian mob. Modeling and simulation of mobbing and swarming implies possibly modeling thousands of independent entities (agents) and is thus well suited for the HPC computational environment.

Current efforts at modeling the battlefield do not do a good job at modeling noncombatant behavior, especially when noncombatants become violent. Human mob modeling is another area that would benefit from HPC support.

Quick-Response Terrorism Modeling Tool Set

Modeling and simulation tools relevant to the war on terrorism are currently handled under separate efforts. For example, genomic and proteomic models are handled by molecular biologists, whereas disease spreading is studied by epidemiologists. HPC can become the catalyst and platform for the integration of many disparate modeling efforts into a coherent, "all-encompassing" quick-response counterterrorism software tool set.

PathSim[9] (Pathogen Simulation) is a computer model of the immune response to viruses developed at Virginia Bioinformatics Institute of Virginia Tech. The creators of the model are trying to incorporate tissue-level modeling and cellular biochemistry simulations then expand to other organs (the respiratory system). We include this as an example of an ongoing effort to integrate separate software tools, which could be relevant to a counterterrorism tool set.

Development and Exploitation of Powerful Visualization Tools

Comparative genomic analysis via visualization of multiple alignments of DNA or RNA sequence data from multiple species is a powerful tool in modern biology. The ability to perform such analyses across an arbitrary number of species, at varying levels of resolution and using phylogenetic[10] trees as guiding frameworks, can be enabled only by HPC.

HPC can also be instrumental in facilitating the difficult task of predicting 3D protein structures. Powerful, HPC-enabled visualization tools can facilitate interactive comparison and analysis of alternative structures. Sophisticated models developed in robotics research and character animation can be used to predict physically meaningful arrangements of groups and clusters of amino acids—a flexible protein backbone and a jointed limb obey the same physics rules.

Finally, the complex dynamical modeling of substrate binding to a protein-ligand site—crucial for a drug correctly docking to its target—could be facilitated within an HPC computational environment.

---

[9] See http://www.research.vt.edu/resmag/fall2004/PathSim.html .

[10] A phylogenetic tree is a diagram that shows the evolutionary relationships and lineages of organisms.

Current Status of Opportunities

The seven proposed novel opportunities for Army HPC in biotechnology and biomedicine are in different stages of development. Some are relying for success on breakthroughs in areas other than high-performance computing. This section ends by briefly reviewing the status of each of these opportunities.

Work to date has demonstrated the feasibility of the concept of biological sentinel using bacteria as the bio-engineered target organisms. Further work is required to achieve a proof of principle eukaryotic sentinel, such as a plant sentinel. The next step will be to make the concept operational within the realm of Army needs. HPC will then be a powerful tool to achieve the design of the required elements as discussed above.

The Theatre Genomic Database method for early detection and identification of biological threats is in the embryonic stage when compared to the more mature DNA analysis tools based on bioagent-specific DNA primers and the Polymerase Chain Reaction. One main issue is whether it is possible to expeditiously generate a theater genomic profile baseline. Questions about how much testing is required before we are confident that the baseline is representative of the *normal* bioagent population can be answered only with thorough experimentation. Furthermore, as already pointed out, implementation of this method requires the transfer of massive amounts of data through secure data links, a challenge that is also faced by current Army efforts that pursue multiple high-fidelity video transmission through wireless networks.

HPC will be the tool of choice for the design of vaccines and immune enhancements for ad hoc biological threats. This opportunity will rely heavily on the continuous progress in the pharmaceutical industry on novel drug design and immune system enhancements. Advancing this concept to the next stage requires a significant breakthrough in reducing the cycle time of drug design and testing or immune enhancement demonstration. Thus, this opportunity is expected to take more time than others to become operational.

The last four Army HPC opportunities have a common denominator, namely, they entail adopting and adapting already existing, state-of-the-art modeling and simulation tools into integrated HPC-based modeling tool sets. None requires scientific or technical breakthroughs to occur, thus, the main limitation to their implementation is the availability of funding. Concerning integration into comprehensive tool sets, it was brought to our attention that quick-response counter terrorism modeling tool sets may be already in development by national laboratories such as Livermore. Those efforts are most likely classified.

CHAPTER FIVE

A Focus on C4ISR Network Modeling and Simulation

The second application focus area we studied was modeling and simulation (M&S) of complex command and control networks involving up to 10,000 mobile wireless nodes on a battlefield.

The key problem with such simulations is line-of-sight (LoS) calculations among all the nodes, whose computation rises as the square of the number of nodes. Figure 5.1 gives an overview of the state of such modeling and simulation. Perhaps a thousand such communicating nodes can be simulated usefully, but with compromises (discussed below). Creating simulations of 10,000 such mobile nodes in a manner that provides useful analytic results for actual battlespace operations is currently beyond the state of the art—but with the continuing exponential growth of HPC (see, for example, the "Top 500" website at http://www.top500.org), it should be achievable within a decade.

Some researchers hope for a breakthrough of sorts in LoS calculations from using specialized graphics CPUs designed and mass-produced for game machines. It is unclear whether the bottleneck of feeding relevant data into and out of these specialized chips will reduce the benefit to a large degree, but continued exploration of this option certainly seems warranted.

A leader within DoD R&D labs in network modeling and simulation is the U.S. Army RDECOM CERDEC at Ft. Monmouth, N.J. We visited Barry Perlman, Monica Farah-Stapleton, and a number of other researchers there in May 2004. One of many charts produced by CERDEC to represent the work under way there is shown in Figure 5.2.

We display this chart to indicate one organization's view on the full range of activities required for C4ISR network analysis, from analysis through modeling and simulation to experimentation, with various feedback loops enriching all activities through what is learned at various stages. In spite of these many analysis and simulation efforts, the problem of accurately modeling thousands of mobile active nodes is still far too difficult for current methodologies. The complexity of the problem is illustrated in Figure 5.3. Here, the U.S. Army's planned Unit of Action (UA) and Unit of Engagement (UE) must coordinate information transmission between moving ground elements and many different air layers.

Simple statistical models have been used to calculate how vertical nodes (unmanned aerial vehicles (UAVs), airships, etc.) have added to network throughput. An example of this using Qualnet is shown in Figure 5.4 for different types of terrain. Far more detailed representations are needed for complex terrain, degraded environmental conditions, and large-scale forces.

Figure 5.1
State of the Art of C2 Network Modeling/Simulation

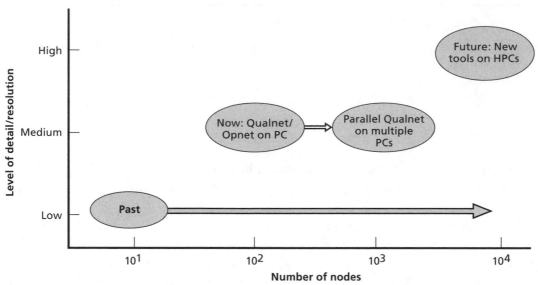

RAND *TR310-5.1*

Modeling and simulation should also be able to inform decisionmakers about trades, such as how options will exhibit different levels of efficiency and robustness. Many different architectures, such as those illustrated in Figure 5.5, have been proposed. Each of these has different responses to node loss, jamming, and other impairments.

These considerations and our examination of HPC (and personal experience with network modeling and simulation (M&S) at RAND) indicate that it is important to distinguish among five levels or "degrees" of network modeling complexity. The first two, where most network modeling occurs now, are low resolution, statistical and medium resolution, routing waveforms. Their attributes are as follows:

- Low resolution, statistical
    — Use a "flat-earth" assumption
    — Have fixed or no attenuations
    — Use a statistical rate of message generation and standard or fixed message lengths
    — Have a fixed ratio of overhead to data messages
- Medium resolution, routing waveforms
    — Often use line-of-sight calculations
    — Use statistical models of attenuation (e.g., Terrain-Integrated Rough Earth Model (TIREM), Irregular Terrain Model (ITM)) over simple terrain
    — Use statistical rate of message generation
    — Use application-layer models of Transmission Control Protocol/Internet Protocol (TCP/IP), User Datagram Protocol (UDP), and other protocols
    — Represent the overhead of routing messages
    — Incorporate antenna models, directional and omnidirectional

Figure 5.2
CERDEC C4ISR Effects M&S Process

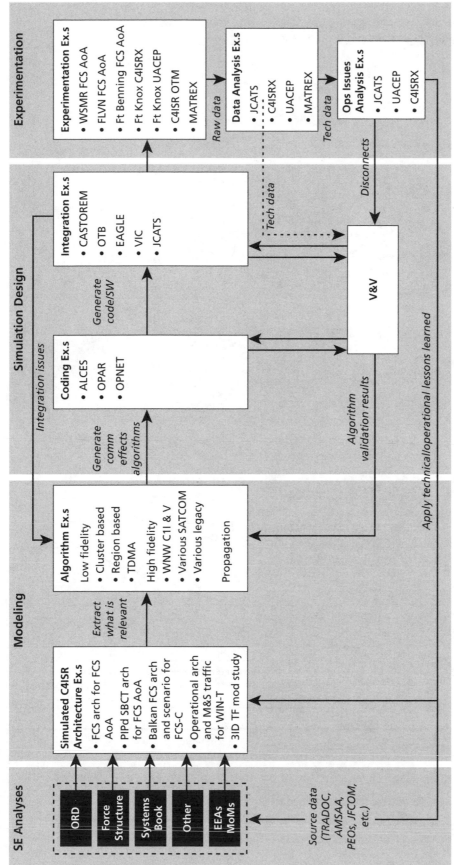

SOURCE: U.S. Army Communications-Electronics RD&E Center (CERDEC), RDECOM.
RAND TR310-5.2

Figure 5.3
Links and Platforms of Future Communications Architectures

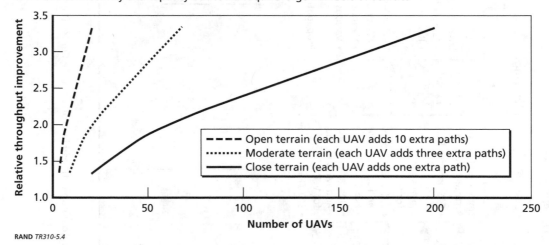

SOURCE: Kioutas (2003).

RAND *TR310-5.3*

Figure 5.4
Effect of Vertical Nodes on Communication Throughput

UAVs add connectivity and capacity but could require large numbers of vehicles

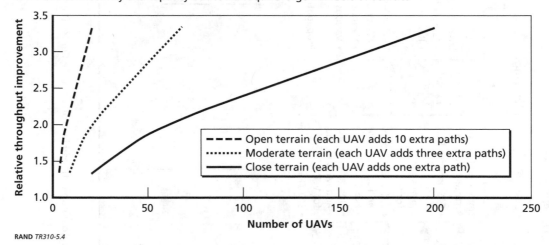

RAND *TR310-5.4*

Figure 5.5
Tradeoff Between Robustness and Efficiency

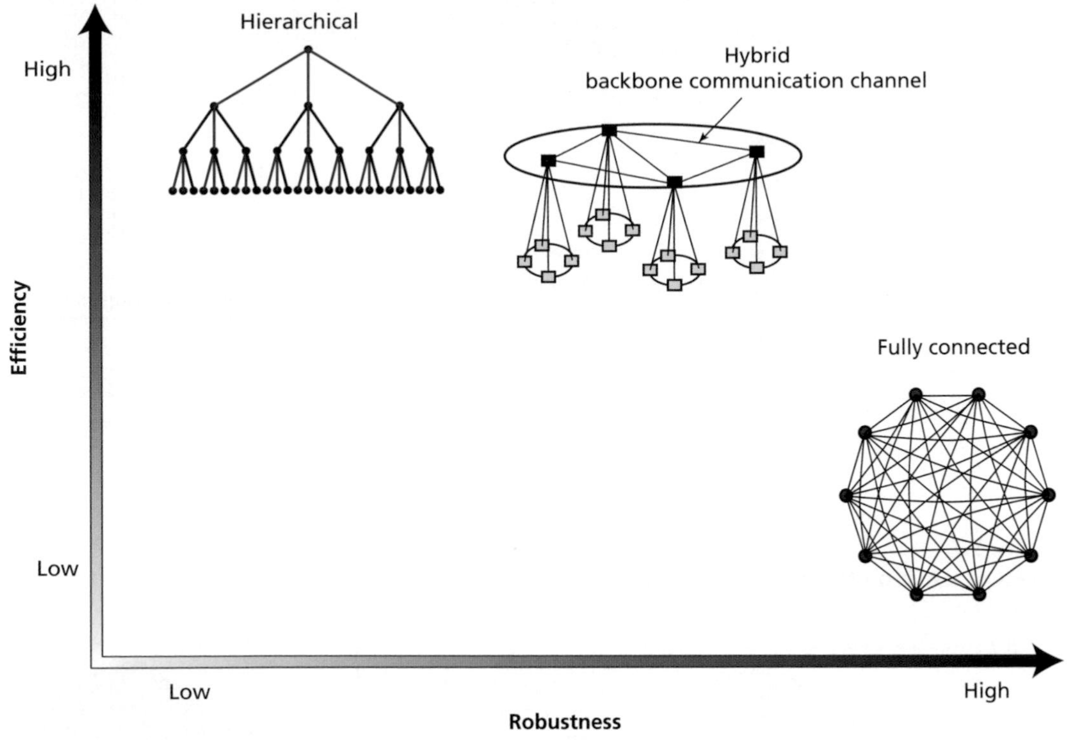

SOURCE: Susan Witty and Isaac Porche (personal communication).
RAND *TR310-5.5*

In general, the compromises made in these levels (e.g., statistical rate of message generation, rather than actual context-dependent battlefield message production) severely limit the utility of these models for operational use or detailed analytical studies. As indicated, most C2 network modeling at present occurs at these two levels. An example of this type of simulation is shown in Figure 5.6. This RAND work characterizes the performance of several different future force communication options. The type of output observed is shown in Figure 5.7. The need for visualization of results is evident even in this simple case.

Levels three and four add force-on-force battle simulations incorporating terrain models and event-driven message generation. At level four, line-of-sight calculations are used to determine exactly which units can communicate with which others and can result in considerable computational burden.

At level five, special models are added to incorporate such complications as noncombatant behaviors, robot planning algorithms, update-in-flight missiles, and so on. The Urban Resolve series of exercises and models are the primary vehicles within which such advanced modeling and simulations are being developed and tested, with a rich graphical interface to display the battlefield environment and the results of the calculations. An image from Phase 1 of Urban Resolve is shown in Figure 5.8, indicating the complexity of the environment being modeled. This first phase involves only sensing of ground elements from some 400 Reconnaissance, Surveillance, and Target Acquisition (RSTA) platforms (no engagement or communications modeling occurs until Phases 2 and 3), but even so it requires extensive supercomputer processing for line-of-sight calculations and after-action review.

Figure 5.6
Example of Qualnet Simulation Experiment

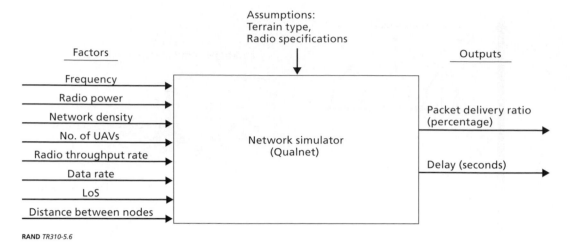

RAND TR310-5.6

Figure 5.7
Effect of UAVs on Network Performance

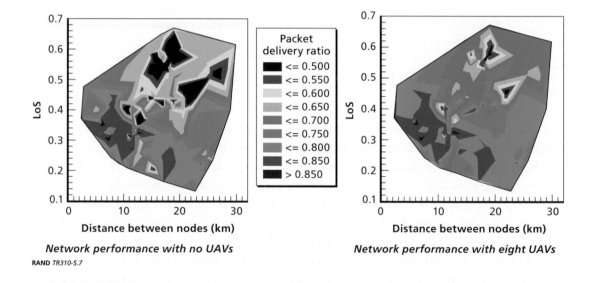

Network performance with no UAVs   *Network performance with eight UAVs*

RAND TR310-5.7

HPC for C2 M&S will increasingly be called on for operational battlefield use, for example, for in-theater planning. Army R&D on C2 M&S should expect the migration of analytic models developed for experimentation into battlefield use (e.g., by transmitting relevant data over high-speed links from the battlefield to CONUS HPC sites), so that communication plans can be resolved overnight as part of planning for the next day's activities.

The main challenges to HPC use for C2 modeling range from getting the physics right for communication models up to coupling simulations with live tests and integration of real-world data, plus visualization tools to understand the complex results emerging from such simulations.

Figure 5.8
Screen Shot from Urban Resolve

SOURCE: Joint Forces Command.
RAND TR310-5.8

In our study of biotech/biomed and C2 networking, we became intrigued by some commonalities across these HPC application areas—commonalities that might be a source of Army R&D that could benefit both fields simultaneously. These commonalities are discussed in the next chapter.

Figure 6.1
Hierarchical Modeling of Structures and Systems

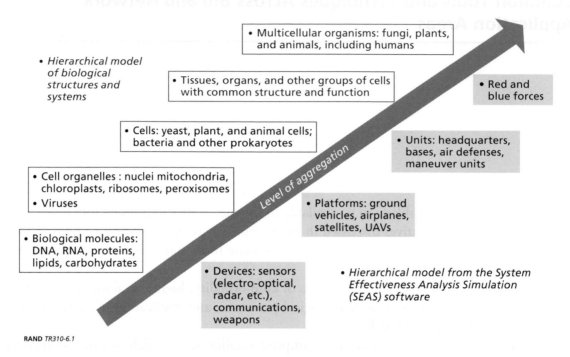

RAND *TR310-6.1*

To the best of our knowledge, defining an M&S taxonomy that depends on level or degree of modeling complexity has not been attempted in the area of biological modeling. We believe that such an attempt would only strengthen this field.

RAND researchers have pioneered the study of "multiresolution" modeling, involving "families of models" that are mutually supportive, for use in the battlefield arena.[2] In this approach, the same physical system is modeled at different levels or degrees of complexity. An attribute or variable defined and operated at a lower resolution level is linked to a set of attributes or variables belonging to higher resolution levels, so that the analyst can access increasing detail starting from the lowest resolution. Imagine the possibilities for Army biological research if an epidemiologist at the U.S. Army MRMC had a software tool that, starting with a top-level schematic of the epidemiology of a particular disease or biological threat, allows him or her to successively access a specific organism, a pathogen, the cell receptor to which that pathogen binds, or the 2D and 3D amino acid structures of both the pathogen and the receptor—both of which will be most likely proteins, etc.

We relate multiresolution modeling to the emerging concept of "systems biology," which promotes these concepts in the specific context of biological sciences.

In hierarchical, or multiresolution, simulations, agent-based concepts are relevant in creating behaviors of larger entities from simpler actions of smaller agents working either independently or in concert.

For many years, biologists have been learning about intracellular transport; cellular organelles; organs; physiology; pathology; and the circulatory, nervous, and immune systems. They have deciphered metabolic and biochemical pathways; reproduced enzymatic reactions in situ (that is, in the laboratory); collected genomic, proteomic, physiologic, and environ-

---

[2] See, for example, Davis and Bigelow (1998); Bigelow and Davis (2003).

mental data on multiple organisms; and assembled all this information into massive databases. However, efforts toward integrating this vast biological knowledge while adding the ability to explain how living beings work as complete systems are relatively recent. The new efforts lie under the umbrella of "systems biology," which deals with studying all the elements of a biological system as a whole, instead of focusing on a single or a small set of genes or proteins. Examples of institutions engaged in this emerging biological field are the Institute for Systems Biology in Seattle, Washington; PNNL in Richland, Washington; and Oak Ridge National Laboratory, Oak Ridge, Tennessee. The Biomolecular Systems Initiative, within PNNL, is part of a larger, DoE-funded effort called "Genomes to Life." Private industry is also starting to show interest in systems biology. For example, Target Discovery, in Palo Alto, California, uses systems biology concepts in drug discovery, and Entelos, in Foster City, California, makes use of systems concepts to devise "PhysioLabs," that is, large-scale models of human disease. Furthermore, HPC is starting to be used in the new field, as exemplified by the affiliation between the Institute for Systems Biology and ARSC at the University of Alaska, Fairbanks. In the future, we can envision the implementation of tools and methods traditionally associated with systems engineering to this emerging field.

In hierarchical or multiresolution simulations, agent-based concepts are relevant in creating behaviors of larger entities from simpler actions of smaller agents working either independently or in concert. Agent-based simulations have enjoyed wide utilization in force-on-force, complex networks; economics; and many other modeling efforts. The Pathogen Simulation software PathSim described in Chapter Four makes use of agent-based concepts. It appears, however, that their use has not been widespread in biological systems research.

The thousands of biochemical reactions that take place inside a cell are organized by biochemists in metabolic pathways. Each pathway consists of a series of consecutive reactions that take certain reactants, go through intermediaries, and generate specific products. Reactants, intermediaries, and products are referred to as metabolites. A distinct protein catalyzes each chemical step of the pathway. Proteins that catalyze biochemical reactions are called enzymes. Figure 6.2 represents the metabolic map—or ensemble of metabolic pathways—for a typical cell. Graph and network theories provide a natural setting to topologically represent the complexity of these maps. We can create a metabolic map by assigning a metabolite to each node and a biochemical reaction (and its corresponding enzyme) to each link or edge. The resulting structure resembles a command and control network.

Even though a metabolic map such as the one shown on Figure 6.2 seems to suggest only static relationships between nodes (metabolites) and edges (biochemical reactions and enzymes), in reality it entails a richness of dynamic interactions, represented by kinetic differential equations that govern the rate of change of concentrations for all the metabolites within the biological system of interest (e.g., a cell). A dynamic model can be embedded in the metabolic map by associating a kinetic equation to each edge using, for example, the well-known (in biochemistry) Michaelis-Menten equation. In its simplest form—a single reactant and a single product—this differential equation is such that at low reactant concentration, the reaction rate—the change of concentration of reactant or product per unit time—is proportional to reactant concentration (linear kinetics), but this rate approaches an asymptotic value as that concentration increases because less and less enzyme is available to

Figure 6.2
Metabolic Pathways

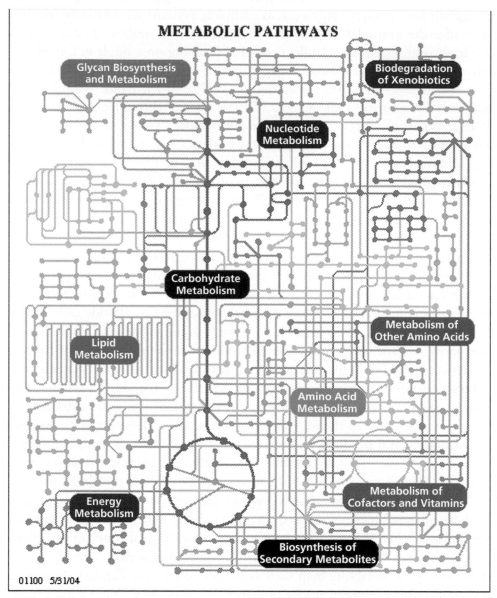

SOURCE: *Kyoto Encyclopedia of Genes and Genomes (KEGG)*, copyright Kanehisa Laboratory.
RAND *TR310-6.2*

catalyze the reaction as more and more enzyme forms a complex with the reactant.[3] The enzymatic mechanism becomes more complicated when the reaction involves multiple reactants or products or when factors external to the reaction—such as pH, that is, concentration of acidic hydrogen—play an important role in the reaction kinetics. Moreover, the thousands of kinetic differential equations associated with the metabolic map are not independent of each other, since numerous feedback mechanisms—notably through enhancers or inhibitors

---

[3] See, for example, Voet and Voet (1995, Chapter 13).

of enzyme action—are at interplay in a typical cell. HPC can therefore become a powerful enabling tool for analyzing a metabolic pathway and solving its associated kinetic equations.

Gene regulatory networks control the level of expression[4] of each gene in a genome. They combine intracellular or extracellular molecular signals, target genes, regulatory proteins called transcription factors, RNA generated from the target genes, and the proteins produced by such RNA. Often they involve complex feedback loops. The modeling of gene regulatory networks is another example of a biological problem that can be analyzed using network concepts, tools, and techniques.

Similar to the case of metabolic maps, gene regulatory networks have associated dynamics, which can be as or more complicated than the sets of coupled Michaelis-Menten differential equations discussed above.[5] In particular, complexity is exacerbated because of the multiple feedback mechanisms occurring in these networks—the product of one gene or set of genes interacts with a completely different gene or set of genes. Hence, HPC can be an indispensable analysis tool for understanding the dynamics of gene regulatory networks.

In general, tools and techniques for handling network analyses in highly parallel HPC computations appear to be relevant in both biological and C2 network modeling; a toolkit of network analysis aids tailored to HPC could well have wide applicability. The relatively new concepts emerging in "the science of networks" could well be applied within this toolkit and prove relevant to a variety of HPC computations.[6]

One of the first questions that arises when analyzing networks is: what is the level of connectivity of the nodes? Otherwise stated, what is the distribution of links per node? Figures 6.2 and 6.3 treat the cases of the metabolic map and gene regulatory network. Similar analyses apply to command and control networks. In the metabolic map, the level of connectivity represents the number of biochemical reactions that each metabolite is involved with. Figure 6.4 shows two extreme cases of node connectivity. Letting P(k) be the distribution of links per node, we see that, at one extreme, P(k) is represented by a Gaussian distribution characterized by the fact that the majority of nodes are approximately "equally connected," whereas at the other extreme, P(k) is given by a power law distribution for which connectivity is very small for the majority of the nodes, with the exception of just a few "super nodes" or "hubs."

It turns out that studies performed on different biological systems demonstrate that such systems tend to follow the power law. Figure 6.5 shows a graph of P(k) for the ubiquitous bacterium E. Coli and a graph of an average P(k).[7] Based on these results, hypotheses have been raised concerning the way that random mutations affect the evolution of biological networks. More work is required to elucidate the consequences of applying these previously not-fully-utilized resources to the biological domain.

The prevalence of the power law in network structures and analysis is common to both biological and C2 networking and is thus relevant in both application domains (as well as others). C2 wireless networks are constrained by line-of-sight problems and electronic war-

---

[4] Gene expression refers to the transcription of the gene from DNA to messenger-RNA and its subsequent translation into protein.

[5] See, for example, Kitano (2001, Chapter 7).

[6] See, for example, Barabási (2002).

[7] Huberman (2001).

Figure 6.3
Gene Regulatory Network for the Sea Urchin

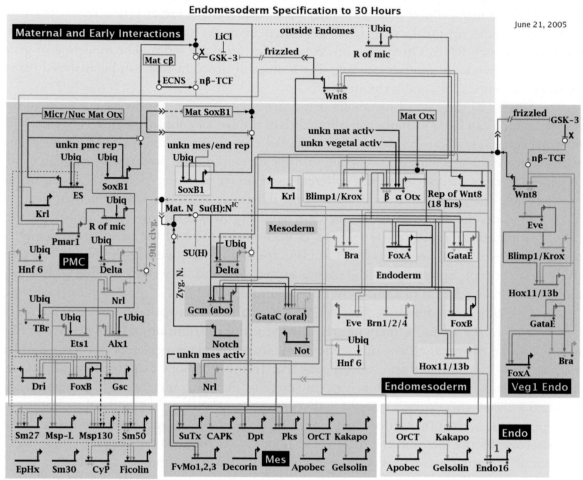

Copyright © 2001–2005, Hamid Bolouri and Eric Davidson.

RAND *TR310-6.3*

fare. These constraints force the networks to evolve toward compartmentalization, with a few critical nodes (hubs) with high connectivity but with most nodes having low connectivity. The result is a network that follows the power law. We note that interesting studies of power law patterns in networks and related mathematical characterizations of them is under way by John Doyle of Caltech and others.[8]

We also note that biological and C2 networking models and simulations are designed and operate at varying degrees of complexity. Table 6.1 compares five levels of complexity between these two application areas. Our point is similar to the one made above, related to hierarchies of models: HPC tools and techniques for modeling and simulation often start with simple levels of complexity, making various statistical simplifying assumptions regarding phenomena being studied. Then these assumptions are gradually replaced with more accurate, real-world data and models, leading to greater complexity and fidelity. This is a

---

[8] Carlson and Doyle (1999); Li et al. (2004).

Figure 6.4
Cases of Node Connectivity

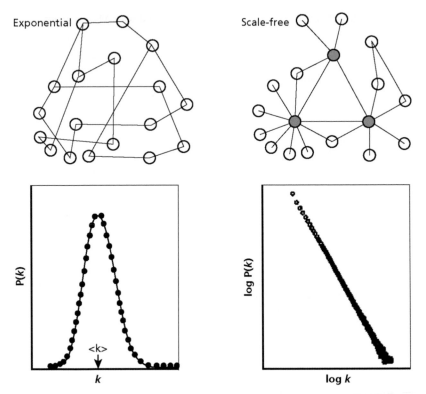

SOURCE: Adapted by permission from MacMillan Publishers Ltd. H. Jeong, B. Tombor,
R. Albert, Z. N. Oltva, and A. L. Barabasi, "The Large Scale Organization of Metabolic
Networks," *Nature*, Vol. 407, 2000, pp. 651–654.

RAND *TR310-6.4*

common enough occurrence in M&S studies that some common tools and techniques for
handling the gradual increase in complexity of HPC models and simulations would seem to
be an important field of study itself. We conclude this discussion with examples of some
tools for an HPC toolkit.

Army R&D HPC researchers would benefit from software tools to help in deciding
the appropriate platform for their computation, given its various attributes. Tools are also
needed to aid in shifting applications among various platform types, not only between vector
and scalar machines but also among PC clusters of varying sizes. Other recommended tools
are interactive interfaces that are independent of particular HPC computer architecture and
visualization tools independent of specific application. These tools are of course more
broadly applicable than just within Army R&D; to the extent possible, they should be developed and promoted in conjunction with such existing programs as the HPCMP Common
HPC Software Support Initiative.

Figure 6.5
P(k) for E. Coli

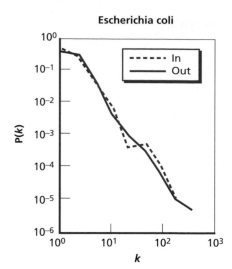
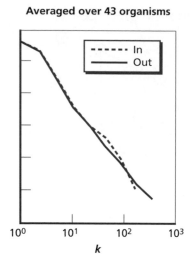

SOURCE: Adapted by permission from MacMillan Publishers Ltd. H. Jeong, B. Tombor, R. Albert, Z. N. Oltva, and A. L. Barabasi, "The Large Scale Organization of Metabolic Networks," *Nature*, Vol. 407, 2000, pp. 651–654. Overlays created by Atul Narang.

RAND *TR310-6.5*

Table 6.1
Parallels Between Bio and C2 Network Modeling Applications

Biotech/biomedical	C2 Network Modeling
1. Statistical modeling of biological or chemical events	1. Low-resolution, statistical
2. Modeling mechanisms for biologic or chemical effects (including protein folding models)	2. Medium-resolution, routing, wave-forms
3. Effects modeling at cellular level (involve agent-based models)	3. Force-on-force
4. Epidemiology of spread of toxins, agents, vectors (involve plume models, behavior-based models)	4. High-resolution, actual messages, dynamic network
5. Expand to include detection of chemical signatures, terrain factors, activity monitoring	5. Add special models

Greater complexity

Additional tools are widely applicable across HPC applications. These include After Action Review tools that collect and organize data and allow tracing of event chains and graphic distribution tools to allow distributed operation of simulations, analyses, and experiments. In our November 2004 workshop, we frequently heard comments about the need for experimental planning aids, so that complex sets of runs (experiments) could be set up, scheduled, and executed without additional human intervention—and preferably could be set to run on a variety of differing architectures and sites (e.g., with varying numbers of PCs in a cluster). Some work in this area is under way in groups concerned with and promoting "grid computing;" Army R&D should monitor and encourage these developments, which are relevant to some of the application areas discussed in this report.

We emphasize that our research on areas of commonality between the modeling of Army wireless networks and of biological systems was motivated by our intention to make recommendations for the funneling of limited Army HPC funding resources. Moreover, we believe that applying network theory concepts as well as various simulation tools (for example, multiresolution modeling) to biological systems modeling and to systems biology has not been fully exploited and would be very illuminating. But by no means do we pretend to suggest that the major issues facing biological systems modeling or systems biology can be resolved by addressing their network content or by analyzing biological problems using exclusively tools from network theory.

CHAPTER SEVEN

Findings

In our study of Army R&D HPC usage, we found a number of favorable aspects. These are listed below.

- Although the Army tends to have fewer HPC projects that use shared HPCMO resources than other services (because it bundles projects into larger ones for ease of administration), it does appear to be getting its "fair share" of DoD HPC cycles (see Figure 3.1).
- We also believe that it is healthy for Army R&D that clusters of computers are becoming relatively inexpensive, allowing individual labs to become initiated into parallel computing with modest clusters (e.g., 16, 32, or 64 CPUs) for development, debugging, and testing of codes. As such applications become more mature, they can then be migrated, as needed, to larger clusters available at MSRCs or distributed SRCs for more substantial runs. Such "democratization" of HPC, however, will entail greater emphasis on training and education, and common software tools support, at diverse R&D sites.
- Other good news in Army (and DoD) R&D HPC involves the DoD HPCMO and its program, HPCMP. These activities provide very substantial support for HPC through major and distributed shared resource centers, and we quite uniformly obtained good reviews of their work, particularly the CHSSI and PET.

The areas we found to be more problematic are listed below.

- The heavy concentration of Army HPC R&D in computational fluid dynamics and armor/projectile/penetration studies, tends to absorb much of the available resources, at the expense of exploration of other, more novel applications (also of great potential benefit to Army operations).
- There is a substantial lack of Army R&D on the important biotech/biomed research areas we listed in Chapter Four. We discuss this further below.
- A set of software tools and techniques appear to have common application within both network and bio modeling, as discussed in Chapter Six. These are worthy of further exploration as a possible focus of Army HPC R&D development.
- As cluster computing spreads to individual labs and agencies, each is in danger of being "below critical mass" in HPC expertise. Furthermore, individual HPC researchers (e.g., software developers) at those sites could well feel the absence of a strong local peer group with whom to share ideas, code, and training. Periodic HPC conferences help in this regard. Such relative isolation may also make recruiting of

HPC experts more difficult than recruiting at major university or commercial labs where there is a greater peer group interested in HPC science and technology.

In the biotech/biomedical focus area we studied, we found Army HPC R&D to be almost nonexistent (we found only four bio-related projects out of 115 in FY 2004)—and those relate primarily to models of dispersion and distribution of biological/chemical agents, not to molecular-level studies.

As mentioned above, the new Biotechnology HPC Software Applications Institute at MRMC is an important development, but it will take years to get fully up to speed on important Army-relevant applications, models, and simulations. It will be important to monitor the institute's efforts at recruiting and hiring, because of the strong demand for HPC-trained biochemists and molecular physicists within the pharmaceutical industry.

We were surprised in our visit to ECBC at Edgewood, Maryland, to find so little activity and interest in high-performance computing. The center's charter is directly relevant to biological applications in rapid development of vaccines and other vital applications, yet much of their work is "wet lab" work that does not develop large amounts of data requiring massive computation and modeling. We hope that the new Biotech HPC SAI at Ft. Detrick, Md., develops ways to tap into the expertise and interests of ECBC researchers as the research program at the new institute is established.

Regarding C2 networking M&S, the framework being developed at CERDEC is impressive and relevant, but because of the scaling problem for line-of-sight calculations especially, a breakthrough appears to be needed in this area. As mentioned above, perhaps use of specialized LoS computational chips being developed for game machines can become relevant, if the data I/O problem can be handled. We found mixed opinions about the likelihood of success in the use of those specialized computational chips.

CHAPTER EIGHT

Recommendations

The Army's Director for Research and Laboratory Management might focus and guide research in novel and vital applications of HPC in many ways. For example, this report has mentioned many biotech/biomedical research areas that appear directly relevant to Army requirements and that would involve the use of high-performance computing.

Resources for new thrusts in Army HPC-related R&D are of course limited. We therefore concentrate on recommendations that could have the broadest effect on a number of Army R&D projects and needs.

First, we recommend that the set of common tools and techniques spanning both the bio and network modeling application areas (discussed in Chapter Six) be considered for funding. These include hierarchical modeling, application of network concepts to biological processes, and application of bio concepts to C2 network modeling. We believe that the fruitful synergies among these areas are worth supporting and will eventually benefit both R&D areas. See, in particular, the discussion of tools for an HPC toolkit in Chapter Six.

Second, we are very impressed with the ability of the HPCMP challenge grants to focus resources and attention on specific areas of DoD interest. ASA(ALT) might consider a smaller, even more focused program patterned after that of the HPCMP, tailored to specific Army requirements. Such challenge grants might also provide incentives for staff crossover between disciplines, such as C2 to bio, visualization to simulations, and fluid dynamics to force-on-force modeling. We do not know the course of development of new graphical processing units, new compression schemes, new cluster architectures, and so forth, so any R&D investment program needs to be flexible, harvesting the best ideas at each step.

Third, consider the concept of an Army-specific "HPC Swat Team" that can focus on a particular laboratory's interests, provide specialized training and education in HPC, help migrate applications from serial to parallel computing architectures, and adapt and use the software tools and toolkits of the CHSSI program within the HPCMP to local applications. After several weeks or months of such intensive support, the team would leave a residual staff behind and then tackle the next lab or agency in need of such focused assistance. Such a team should also be supplemented by a "help line" and consulting services for those organizations with other HPC-related needs. The purpose of this recommendation is to address the growing use of "home-grown" HPC within individual labs (e.g., using small- to medium-sized clusters) and having less-than-critical-mass expertise in HPC within those separate labs and agencies.[1] (We are aware that the ARL provides some of these activities; we believe that these efforts need to be expanded, either by ARL or by others.)

Fourth, in general, support the use of cluster computing for HPC within individual labs and agencies. These provide valuable hands-on HPC expertise and allow the migration, development, and debugging of HPC-related codes in a more interactive, intensive manner than submitting batch jobs to an MSRC. As stated above, this trend does not take away from the important resource that the MSRCs and distributed centers provide, because major "runs" of code after debugging would most likely be done in their much more substantial facilities.

Fifth, focus attention on what we have called "conceptual, tactical, and cultural problem areas" (see the discussion of challenges in Chapter Three). End-users or customers of Army R&D have often asked, "Why is HPC needed for this?" "Will the resulting HPC-driven models and simulations replace any field testing?" "What is the business case for using HPC, as opposed to our normal methods?" Someone within the Army lab system should be tasked to compile lessons learned, analyses, and accurate data and logic stating *when* HPC is best used, *how* it will affect outcomes, and *why* it is worthwhile in particular application areas. These questions are apparently encountered often enough that guidance and support for answering them are needed.

Last, we recommend that the Army make a request of the HPCMP to add one or two CTAs to their existing list (or else recast some existing ones). The purpose is to give prominence and focus to the areas of biotech/biomed R&D and network modeling and simulation (with special attention to large-scale mobile communication networks). At present, these R&D application areas are scattered among a number of CTAs.

The above recommendations are aimed at focusing incremental Army R&D HPC activities, in addition to the substantial and important work already under way in more traditional areas such as computational fluid dynamics and projectile/armor impact studies. Of all our recommendations, we call special attention to the idea of promoting and funding HPC tools and techniques that can span both biotech/biomed and communication network simulation applications. Some suggestions for such tools are listed in Chapter Six, but we believe further study and elaboration of these ideas would be important for the Army R&D HPC community.

---

[1] We note that this recommendation is somewhat controversial. Others have mentioned that it is unclear what residual would be left behind as a result of this effort. Additionally, cultural change in the organizations receiving such assistance may be necessary, with more emphasis on their hiring relevant scientific talent within the Army laboratories.

Appendix

November 17, 2004, Army R&D HPC Workshop

Participants (Presenters in bold)
AHPCRC
Muzio, Paul
Kumar, Vipin
Namburu, Raju
AMRDEC
Ray, Teddy
AMSAA
Chizmar, Steven
ARDEC
Albinson, George
Dyer, Jeff
ARL (including MSRC)
Breaux, Harold
Forch, Brad
Gowens, John
Hurley, Margaret
Kimsey, Kent
Nietubicz, Charles
Zoltoski, Mike
ARO
Reynolds, Peter
ASA(ALT)
Barnette, Ken
Beatrice, Pamela
Nash, Carolyn
Parmentola, John

CERDEC

Farah-Stapleton, Monica
Rhodes, David

DARPA

Shaffer, Dolores (SETA to Bob Graybill)

ERDC

Holland, Jeff
Maier, Robert

Hewlett-Packard

Briggs, Steve
Soldwedel, Joy

HPCMO

Henry, Cray
Mark, Andy

HPCMO PET FMS

Pratt, David

IDA (representing JFCOM J9)

Graebener, Bob

MRMC

Reifman, Jaques

PEO STRI

Macedonia, Michael

RAM Labs, Inc.

Steinman, Jeffrey

RAND

Anderson, Robert
Bonds, Tim
Hearn, Tony
Horn, Ken
Lewis, Rosalind
Pfleeger, Shari Lawrence
Steeb, Randall

RDECOM Headquarters

Byers, Jack
Jenkins, Bob

Scalable Networks Technologies	
	Bagrodia, Rajive

SMDC	
	McBride, Marshall

TARDEC	
	Kedziorek, Daniel

USC/ISI	
	Lucas, Bob

Agenda:

Time	Item	Presenter
0800	*Complementary rolls, coffee, juice*	
0830	**Introductory remarks**	John Parmentola, ASA(ALT)
0900	**Self-introductions of participants ("around the table")**	
0925	**Description of RAND Arroyo Center HPC project—goals, approach, activities**	Robert Anderson, RAND
0940	**Current Army R&D involving HPC—four examples**	
	Command and control simulations involving 10K+ mobile entities	Monica Farah-Stapleton, CERDEC
	Future force modeling for survivability and lethality	Kent Kimsey, ARL
	Biotechnology HPC Software Applications Institute—Defense against chemical warfare agents (CWAs) and toxic industrial chemicals (TICs)	Jaques Reifman, MRMC Margaret Hurley, ARL
1045	*Break*	
1100	**What's going on elsewhere? Examples of HPC developments and usage of potential relevance**	
	DARPA High Productivity Computing Systems program; AHPCRC/ARL research and collaborations in exploiting HPC	Dolores Shaffer, DARPA (SETA) Vipin Kumar, AHPCRC
1140	**Some results from survey of Army HPC usage and projections (HPCMP data)**	Rosalind Lewis, RAND
1200	*Lunch*	
1300	**DoD-wide HPC facilities and plans in HPCMP**	Cray Henry, HPCMP
1320	**Army HPC facilities and plans**	Charlie Nietubicz, ARL MSRC and AHPCRC Jeff Holland, ERDC

1400	**Discussion: What are the greatest HPC missing opportunities for Army R&D?**	
1445	*Break*	
1500	**Discussion: What are the key roadblocks to more effective HPC usage for Army R&D?**	
1600	**Discussion: What should SAALT do to promote more effective HPC usage for Army R&D?**	
1645	**Concluding remarks**	John Parmentola, ASA(ALT)
1700	*End of workshop*	

Bibliography

Baker, Mark, and Rajkumar Buyya, "Cluster Computing at a Glance," in Rajkumar Buyya, ed., *High Performance Cluster Computing*, Vol. 1, Upper Saddle River, N.J.: Prentice Hall PTR, 1999, pp. 3–47.

Barabási, Albert-László, *Linked: The New Science of Networks*, Cambridge, Mass.: Perseus Publishing, 2002.

Bigelow, J. H., and Paul K. Davis, *Implications for Model Validation of Multi-Resolution Multiperspective Modeling (MRMPM) and Exploratory Analysis,* Santa Monica, Calif.: RAND MR-1750-AF, 2003.

Bobayashi, H., et al., "Programmable Cells: Interfacing Natural and Engineered Gene Networks," *PNAS*, Vol. 101, No. 22, 2004.

Boris, Jay, et al., "Simulation of Fluid Dynamics Around Complex Urban Geometries," *Proceedings of the 39th Aerospace Sciences Meeting, American Institute of Aeronautics and Astronautics*, Reston, Va., 2001.

Carlson, J. M., and J. Doyle. "Highly Optimized Tolerance: A Mechanism for Power Laws in Designed Systems," *Physical Review E,* Vol. 60, No 2, August 1999, pp. 1412–1427.

Clarke, J. A., "Emulating Shared Memory to Simplify Distributed-Memory Programming," *IEEE Computing in Science and Engineering*, Vol. 4, No. 1, January–March 1997, pp. 55–62.

Computing Research Association, Workshop on the Roadmap for the Revitalization of High-End Computing, Washington, D.C.: Computing Research Association, June 16–18, 2003.

Davis, Paul K., and J. H. Bigelow, *Experiments in Multiresolution Modeling*, Santa Monica, Calif.: RAND MR-1004-DARPA, 1998.

Davis, Paul K., and Robert H. Anderson, *Improving the Composability of Department of Defense Models and Simulations*, Santa Monica, Calif.: RAND MG-101-OSD, 2003.

Defense Technical Information Center, *Developing Critical Technologies, Section 3—Biological Technology*, 2003. Online at www.dtic.mil/mctl.

Department of Defense, *Requirements Questionnaire, High Performance Computing Modernization Program.* Online at http://www.hpcmo.hpc.mil/Htdocs/Require/index.html.

Federal Plan for High-End Computing, Report of the High-End Computing Revitalization Task Force (HECRTF), NCO/IT R&D, Washington, D.C., May 10, 2004

Ferber, D., "Synthetic Biology: Microbes Made to Order," *Science*, Vol. 303, No. 5655, 2004, pp. 158–161.

Gerchman, Y., and R. Weiss, "Teaching Bacteria a New Language," *PNAS*, Vol. 101, No. 8, 2004, pp. 2221–2222.

http://bfi.org/node/380 .

Huberman, B. A., *The Laws of the Web: Patterns in the Ecology of Information*, Cambridge, Mass.: MIT Press, 2001.

Hwang, K., and Z. Xu, *Scalable Parallel Computing: Technology, Architecture, Programming*, New York: WCB/McGraw-Hill, 1998.

Jeong, H., B. Tombor, R. Albert, Z. N. Oltva, and A. L. Barabasi, "The Large Scale Organization of Metabolic Networks," *Nature,* Vol. 407, 2000, pp. 651–654.

Information Assurance Technology Analysis Center (IATAC), *Exploring Biotechnology Opportunities for the Department of Defense (Released from the Director of Net Assessment) Critical Review & Technology Assessment (CR/TA) Report*, Washington, D.C., 2002.

Kioutas, N., *Airborne Communications Newsletter*, September 29, 2003.

Kitano, H., ed., *Foundations of Systems Biology*, Cambridge, Mass.: MIT Press, 2001.

Kyoto Encyclopedia of Genes and Genomes (KEGG), Tokyo: Kanehisa Laboratories.   Online at http://www.genome.ad.jp/kegg/, accesed December 15, 2005.

Li, L., D. Alderson, W. Willinger, and J. Doyle. "A First-Principles Approach to Understanding the Internet's Router-Level Topology," Association for Computing Machinery, *SIGCOMM Computer Communication Review*, Vol. 34, No. 4, October 2004.

Looger, L., et al., "Computational Design of Receptor and Sensor Proteins with Novel Functions," *Nature*, Vol. 423, 2003, pp. 185–189.

Manzardo, Mark A., and Kenneth G. LeSueur, "An Infrared-Scene Projector Digital Model," *Computing in Science and Engineering*, March–April 2002, pp. 58–65.

National HPCC Software Exchange, *High Performance Computing and Communications Glossary,* Syracuse, N. Y.: Syracuse University. Online at http://www.npac.syr.edu/nse/hpccgloss/hpccgloss.html#S.

Peterkin, Robert E., and John W. Luginsland, "A Virtual Prototyping Environment for Directed-Energy Concepts," *Computing in Science and Engineering*, March–April 2002, pp. 42–49.

Porche, Issac, Lewis Jamison, and Tom Herbert, "Framework for Measuring the Impact of C4ISR Technologies and Concepts on Warfighter Effectiveness Using High Resolution Simulation," 2004. Online at http://www.dodccrp.org/events/2004/CCRTS_San_Diego/CD/papers/233.pdf.

Post, Douglas E., "The Coming Crisis in Computational Science," Keynote Address, IEEE International Conference on High Performance Computer Architecture: Workshop on Productivity and Performance in High-End Computing, Madrid, Spain, February 14, 2004, Los Alamos Report LA-UR-04-0388. Online at http://www.tgc.com/hpcwire/hpcwireWWW/04/0319/107234.html and http://www.hpcwire.com/hpcwire/hpcwireWWW/04/0326/107294.html.

Schraml, Stephen J., Kent D. Kimsey, and Jerry A. Clarke, "High Performance Computing Applications for Survivability-Lethality Technologies," *Computing in Science and Engineering*, March–April 2002, pp. 16–21.

Third International Symposium on High Performance Distributed Computing, San Francisco, Calif., August 2–5. Online at http://cell-relay.indiana.edu/mhonarc/cell-relay/1994-May/msg00213.html.

U.S. Department of Commerce, *A Survey of the Use of Biotechnology in Industry*, Washington, D.C., October, 2003.

Voet, Donald, and Judith Voet, *Biochemistry*, New York: John Wiley & Sons, 1995.

Warner, Col. J., et al., "Exploring Biotechnology: Opportunities for the Department of Defense," *Critical Review and Technology Assessment Report*, Washington, D.C.: IATAC, 2002.

Zimmerman, Z., M. Swenson, and J. Golden, "Biodefense: Novel DNA Analysis Technologies for Next-Generation Early Warning Biodetection Systems and Their IT Implications," *IDC*, Vol. 1, No. 31332, May 2004.